William Jennings Bryan Oleander's

GUIDE TO KANSAS

HOW YOU KNOW WHEN YOU'RE HERE

By Thomas Fox Averill

Illustrated by Patrick Marrin

Printed in the United States of America
by Mennonite Press, Inc.

ISBN 1-880652-88-9

Edited by Diane Samms Rush

Dedication

This book is dedicated to dinner tables everywhere,
particularly the one where
Stuart Carson Averill
(1924-1996)
so enjoyed the exercise of opinion
and where
Elizabeth "Tucker" Averill
showed how opinion might be sharpened with wit.
Both of these people guided me to Here.

Introduction

I am pleased to contribute a few thoughts about this new *Guide to Kansas,* written by one of the most astute Kansas observers, William Jennings Bryan Oleander, of Here, KS. Those of us who are Here don't often wonder where we are, but the book provides some very helpful guidelines for our visitors and recent transplants, and reminds all of us about what is most important about being Here.

Oleander captures some of the essence and strange quirks about living in Kansas. He talks about what Kansans love and what we don't trust, and what Kansans hold in common.

As an elected official, when I want to find out what voters are thinking, listening to Oleander's commentary on the radio is more helpful to me than listening to the words of country music songs or the themes of TV evangelists, which were two sources I've always trusted more than most polls.

Oleander reminds us that, most of all, Kansans must keep a sense of humor. He pokes good-natured fun at symbols which have taken on inflated importance, and makes us think about what's important to treasure.

If you read *Oleander's Guide to Kansas,* and find yourself chuckling out loud, if it helps you remember your favorite neighbor or your grandpa, if you rethink a few political issues, then you'll know you're Here. Or if you're there, you'll wish you were Here, with us.

—*Kathleen Sebelius, Insurance Commissioner, State of Kansas*

Preface

Almost ten years ago I created William Jennings Bryan Oleander as the main character of a novel. A retired farmer, he was sick of seeing Kansas and American agriculture and culture replaced by the agribusiness and retail chains: ADM-Farmland- J.C.-Crown-Mc-Hut-Mart-Max, Ltd. Mr. Oleander lived in an older Kansas, both in spirit and in truth, both historically and culturally, and was fiercely loyal to both its strengths and weaknesses.

Although my novel had a definite character, it had no plot, and I put it aside. Then Wichita's Ks. Magazine began publication, and I wrote letters to the editor, by William Jennings Bryan Oleander, from the "real Kansas"—from the little town of Here. Other characters began to populate Here, and Near Here, and finally There. By 1990 I had found in Oleander a way to express much of my knowledge and intuitions about Kansas, through humor and satire, through the barbed comment. Oleander was an outlet for me.

I had just edited *What Kansas Means to Me: Twentieth Century Writers on the Sunflower State* (University Press of Kansas), which gathered together a group of affectionate essays exploring the meaning and appeal of Kansas. I have always taught Kansas Literature, Folklore and Film at Washburn University of Topeka, trying my best to excite students about the place where they live. I have tried hard to be a positive ambassador for Kansas. The Oleander character allowed me to jab, punch, poke and deflate, to explore the hypocrisies, the contradictory history, the sagging cultural images, the lack of truth-telling in governments and chambers of commerce, all through someone like, but not like, myself.

In 1990, I approached KANU-91.5, Public Radio from the University of Kansas, with the idea of turning Mr. Oleander into a radio commentator. I auditioned, and have been assuming Oleander's gravelly Kansas voice ever since: monthly, then every two weeks, then once a week during the 1995 and 1996 legislative sessions, after Oleander (D-Here) was elected to the

Kansas Statehouse for one term.

This book is my attempt to bring together those commentaries that distill the Kansas of William Jennings Bryan Oleander. I call it a "guide" because it seeks to inform, instruct and to lead you into a Kansas that is both fictional (from Here to There) and historical (from Coronado's guide to Joan Finney's harp). The 34 short chapters (Kansas was the 34th state to enter the Union) begin with Oleander's take on history, culture and place, and end with the more personal accounts of his life in Here, Kansas.

No preface would be complete without gratitude. I thank, first and foremost, Jeffrey Ann Goudie, who has always been my best reader, editor and critic; I am doubly lucky in that she is also my wife. Howard Hill and many other fine people at KANU- 91.5 FM in Lawrence helped Oleander find a wide radio audience. Cliff Hall, of the Topeka Metro News, on the urging of Bill Craven, put Oleander in print from the beginning. Washburn University has generously given me both the time and the facilities to continue my Oleander commentaries, especially during the legislative sessions. And, though too numerous to name, Oleander's truest support has come from all the listeners and readers who have offered criticism, suggestions and compliments. Thanks to everyone who has written, phoned, or approached me, asking that I relay greetings to Mr. William Jennings Bryan Oleander of Here, Kansas. Both of us are fed by Kansans, as well as by our mutual relationship.

Thomas Fox Averill
WASHBURN UNIVERSITY OF TOPEKA

Contents

ix

ON KANSAS

ON AGE AND LOVE

Here, Kansans Live in Small Towns

There is no place in the world where nomenclature is so rich, poetical, humorous, and picturesque as in the United States of America.
        —*Robert Louis Stevenson*

There is probably no state in the union with such a rich variety of place-names as the state of Kansas.

        —*John Rydjord,*
        Kansas Place-Names

Folks, I'm William Jennings Bryan Oleander. The William Jennings Bryan is for the great "Boy Orator of the Platte," the great "Popocrat" (half Populist/half Democrat), the People's Hope at the turn of the century in the presidential election of 1896, when it looked for a hopeful moment like the common people might grab control from the moneyed, self-interested corporations. I'm proud of my name.

So what if William Jennings Bryan lost in 1896? And again in 1900? And in 1908? So what if Bryan went from great political orator, to Chautauqua lecturer, to honorary prosecutor of that evolution-teaching John T. Scopes in the great Scopes Monkey Trial? So what that Bryan was mercilessly upstaged by Clarence Darrow? So what, in short, if Bryan was best known for his repeated failure to become president and his failure to return a Creator/God to the schools before his death in 1925, five days after the Monkey trial? I'm still named after a famous man: just ask my daddy, Abraham Lincoln Oleander.

Not a one of us Oleanders knows where the

Oleander comes from. We know the oleander is a plant; we know it grows well in Kansas; we know it's poisonous in all its parts: berry, leaf, stem, branch and root. Has that shaped me and my kin? Well, we speak our minds; we let folks chew into us and spit us back out; we grow where we're set without fear of enemies; we're not nourishing but we have our beauty, our elegance, our place in the world, and in Kansas.

And since the early days of the state, that place has been Here, Kansas. Now don't go hustling to find your latest Kansas Department of Transportation map of the Sunflower State: You won't find Here, Kansas.

Who would want to get here? A failed bank and a closed-down post office share the same old limestone building. To get a money order, you drive over to Near Here (don't look for it on the map, either) and see Harvey O'Connell at the Near Here Tavern and Mini-skirt Museum (don't get too excited—it's just one mini- skirt that young Harv scavenged from that bus wreck in 1972).

Everything else we need is in Here. Young Claude Hopkins down at the Mini-Mart will cash a Social Security check. The Here, Kansas, Co-op has a screen door and a flyswatter in the summer, a woodstove and a checkerboard in the winter. Elmer Peterson's Drive-Thru Pharmacy and Car Wash keeps us clean and medicated. You see, most of us in Here are what you'd call over the hill, only there aren't any hills out here to be over. Why, it's so flat you can stand on tiptoe and see grain elevators in five surrounding counties.

Our tallest citizen is Barney Barnhill. We call him the "Weatherman" because he's so tall he sees storms rolling in five or ten minutes before the rest of us. Barney runs Here's great tourist attraction, the Demolition Derby Museum, open from 3:45 to 5:00 the first and fourth Friday of most months, and 8:00 until closing every other Saturday except in months beginning with "J" and "A." Come see us. Barney will talk your ear off about the history of those Kansas Demolition Derby Circuit cars.

Folks, for the last several years, since I turned ninety, I've been the honorary Mayor of Here. We used to elect someone, until election expenses became our entire budget. Plus the drawback of working with Hattie and Tommy Burns. They're the cultural sector of Here, Kansas. She's a hairdresser. He repaired speedboats until Here Lake dried up. Together, they run the Here College of Beauty and Fiberglass Maintenance. They're Here boosters. Once a year they put an ad for Here and the College in the Wichita paper, then sit back waiting for a rush of discontented city folks. When nobody shows up, they get mad and try to charge the ad to the city. It's my job to say, "Nope, Here won't pay."

You see, Here, Kansas, was founded when a bunch of our ancestors strayed from the Santa Fe Trail. They didn't know where they were going. They were as whiney as a bunch of kids. "Are we here yet?" they kept asking the wagonmaster. Finally, he sneaked away one night. They weren't smart enough to know they'd been abandoned. They thought they'd arrived. They called the place Here, and we've been here ever since.

In the early days, we boosted the town, took ads in the Eastern papers, brought in reporters from Topeka, lied ourselves red-faced for nothing. Every one of us traces our heritage to that original wagon train. If you can't find us on the map, that's okay; we've been lost most of our history. And being lost means we haven't often been found. Think about that advantage: We haven't found crime, nor welfare, nor teenage pregnancy (try to find a teenager in Here!), nor local car dealer commercials, nor Kiwanis clubs, nor salad bars, nor a sign on the highway that reads "Welcome to Here, Kansas, Population 38."

But being lost also means we've remained true Kansans: unadorned, unalloyed Kansans. Here is the unvarnished truth about Kansas, without the propaganda of state government, economic development, or the Kansas Department of Commerce, Travel and Tourism.

Let me give you an example: You know how state officials are always talking about something they call Brain Drain? Of course the politicians want you to think Kansas has Brain Drain because our kids leave the state after a stint in one of our Margin of Average colleges. But in Here, we see Brain Drain from the local view. For lots of us, Brain Drain is a personal problem. And we don't get it from leaving the state. Hell, we get it from staying. And Here is the only Kansas community doing something about it.

You see, back toward the end of W.W. Two, J.W. Small needed help. J.W. and his wife, Minnie Small, were set to adopt a war baby, clear from France. Folks in Here had never seen an honest-to-God French person—Frogs, they called them back then—let alone a tadpole. The whole town was ready to welcome that baby when J.W. panicked. Held a town meeting. Invited a professor from a junior college two counties over. J.W. told us what was wrong. The professor laughed, told J.W. he didn't have to learn French, the baby'd start right out talking English.

"How can it be?" asked J.W. "The baby's French. Says so on the papers." J.W. only wrote a thank-you to that egghead professor after the baby started right out speaking American. First words: "No" and "wee wee" (he was a little pisser).

So, in 1944, J.W. founded the first group in Kansas to recognize Brain Drain. He called it DENSA, a support group for thick skulls, slow thinkers, numbskulls; for the dull-witted, dizzy, and dense. To join, you just confess you've got a drained brain, then try to remember when the meetings are. Our mascot is the scarecrow from The Wizard of Oz: his head may be stuffed with straw, but at least he has something up there.

Now, DENSA likes to keep busy. I'll give you a for instance. Pierre Small, who has grown up to be our lifetime president, became very worried when one of our citizens, Fred Pete, died recently, leaving behind a blind dog, whose name is Revor—that's Rover spelled backwards.

Pierre went around with a sign-up sheet, asking everyone in Here to take a turn as a seeing-eye person for that blind dog. He wanted folks to make sure the dog didn't get run over crossing the street. Folks willing to spot a cat or two. Or a fresh load of garbage. "A dog," Pierre told me, "oughta be able to be a dog, even if it is blind."

"That's right," I said, and signed up for an hour.

"Make sure you do dog things," he said.

"Don't worry," I said, "I know where every fire hydrant in Here is, and if we run out, I'll take him to Near Here."

But Pierre didn't stop there. Why, one

afternoon Pierre was almost run over by a lost truck. His eyes were squeezed shut. "Watch where you're going!" I shouted at him.

"Is that you, William?" he asked.

"Open your eyes."

"I can't," he said. "This is part of my sensitivity training. If I'm going to be a seeing-eye person for Revor, I've got to feel how hard it is to be blind."

"Where's that darn dog now?" I asked.

"I don't know," Pierre admitted. "I lost him."

"And you're looking for him with your eyes closed?"

"See what I mean, William," said Pierre, finally opening his eyes. "Do you see how hard it is to be blind?"

Lord, folks, when I saw Pierre next, he'd finally found the dog. He was practically dragging Revor down the street.

"Frustrated?" I asked him.

"Darn and mon dieu," he said. "I swear this dog is so blind it doesn't know where it wants to go."

Folks, you could say the same about DENSA, and maybe about Here. But that's only if you're an outsider. We insiders aren't afraid to be who we are: Kansans; Here, Kansans; lifetime DENSA members.

7

Here, Kansans Know Their History

> *Until 1895 the whole history of the state was a series of disasters, and always something new, extreme, bizarre, until the name Kansas became a byword, a synonym for the impossible and the ridiculous, inviting laughter, furnishing occasion for jest and hilarity.* —Carl Becker, "Kansas"

Nobody will tell you the truth about Kansas quicker than an old Here, Kansan like me. You know, back in the early days, teachers took a test to prove their knowledge of Kansas history. Before they were allowed in a one-room school to be terrorized by gangly farm boys, they had to correctly answer such questions as, "What was the Andover Band?"

Maybe that standard was a little high. But later, the teaching of Kansas history was dropped from the curriculum altogether. State pride plummeted until a majority of Kansans were shocked that our kids didn't know the difference between a Bushwhacker and a Jayhawker: They thought a Jayhawk was a tall fellow who played basketball well enough to be on the TV.

So the Kansas Legislature mandated that the schools teach Kansas history, at least a unit, sometime, in one of the grades, like it or not. Administrators tried to figure out how to sneak it in so it wouldn't take up much time, and, God forbid, so they didn't have to hire anybody new.

Teachers tore their hair out looking for materials. Academics at the state colleges produced books and articles and resource packets to fill the void.

Folks, Kansans should know their history. But there must be a middle ground between total ignorance and an intimate knowledge of the Andover Band. Just what should a Kansan know? Well, here's the DENSA Society version, written by some of us who have lived through a lot Kansas history:

First, Coronado killed the Indian who lured him here talking about the seven cities of gold. Everybody's been disappointed with Kansas ever since, except for the buffalo, and we killed all of them but for a few out by Garden City, and except for the Indians, only we killed a bunch of them, too, and sent the rest to Oklahoma.

After that, we fought the Bushwhacking Missouri slavers and became "Bleeding Kansas," killed a lot of folks just trying to keep slavery out, then wrote Blacks out of the Kansas constitution altogether.

We wanted Kansas to be a Free State, so after the Civil War, we gave most of our Kansas land away to the Union Army veterans and the Kansas Pacific and Santa Fe railroads. We even gave some to the Exodusters, those Black migrants from the South, so we could show African Americans how Southern we were after all.

Then Kansas got a bunch of other immigrant groups, including the Russian-Germans, who brought Turkey Red Winter Wheat and made us the Wheat State. We suffered grasshoppers, droughts, blizzards and every other Biblical plague. We even suffered the cowboys long enough to get Dodge City on the TV later.

We came out of the 1880s poor and crazy, we prohibited liquor and gambling, and we started after the railroads. We gave power to the scraggly farmers in the Populist Party just long enough for William Allen White to get famous writing "What's the Matter with Kansas?" even though everyone had known what was wrong since Coronado—and not being able to fortify with a stiff drink didn't help.

We joined up with the Progressive movement so we could stay Republican—even through the Great Depression and the New Deal.

We didn't leave during the Dust Bowl, not being as smart as the Okies, who went to California and made sure their kids could drink good wine and sit around in hot tubs.

Alf tried to be President, did about as well as most Kansans do at anything, and so we honor him.

Then there was Ike—a war hero, good at campaigns, with a nice smile. A true Kansan—he looked like Grandpa on downers—so we finally got us a President, and a library.

That's it, except when the Clutters got killed and Dorothy started getting on the TV every year.

And the Andover Band? Beats the heck out of me. But don't worry, you'll be able to pass as a Kansan without knowing that one.

Here, Kansans Know Their State Symbols

TORNADO
If it hadn't been for the storms
We'd have had nothing
to talk about.

—Dallas Wiebe,
The Kansas Poems

Like our history, our state symbols pretty much tell us about Kansas and Kansans: history, geography, culture. Every good Kansan will keep them in mind, and I make sure that each January 29th I call my grandson. You see, he was raised in Kansas, but after getting a pretty good education at one of our Margin of Average Universities here, he moved away and only comes back for visits.

"Happy Kansas Day!" I greet him.

"What?" he asks, the line crackling with California static.

"Happy Kansas Day," I say. "It's January 29th. Do you know how old Kansas is?" I ask.

He is always silent.

"You have to know just what year Kansas became which state," I remind him.

More silence.

Then I do the math for him, and tell him how old. "Kansas entered the Union in 1861, to become the 34th state," I say. "And do you know which president Eisenhower was? That's 34th, too."

"No," he says. "I didn't know. Or else I've

forgotten."

Folks, if you want to be a Here, Kansan, you have to know the basics. You have to identify with Kansas. It's no wonder so many young people up and leave. Just to prove my point, I quiz my grandson on the state symbols and he misses two out of three. Most Kansans these days can't do much better:

1. State Motto?
2. State Animal?
3. State Bird?
4. State Song?
5. State Flower?
6. State name means?
7. State March?
8. State Banner?
9. State Tree?
10. State Nicknames?
11. State Insect?
12. State Reptile?
13. State Amphibian?
14. State Soil?

"Those are the official symbols, written into the law books in Topeka," I tell my grandson.

"Topeka," I remind him, "is the State Capital."

"I know that," he sighs. "Isn't this call costing you money?"

He's right for the first time all day, and I hang up, still full of the state symbols. You know, I'm always glad when the schoolkids campaign for a new symbol, like the honeybee in '76, and the ornate box turtle in '86. Fact is, I think we need even more of them, to let ourselves and others in on what it is to be Kansans. So here are some nominations:

For the State Weather: the Tornado.

For the State Greeting: the Western Kansas One-finger Salute (the finger raised slightly from the hand on the top of the steering wheel).

For the State Headwear: the Feed Cap.

For the State Modifier: the word "Pretty," as in "pretty much."

For the State Sentence Opener: the word "Well," as in, "Well, what do you know?"

For the State Affirmation: "Yep."

For the State Negative: "Nope."

For the State Scenery: Level.

Now here's how these symbols would work:

Let's say it's the day after a devastating tornado, and two Kansas farmers give a one-finger greeting and stop their pickup trucks to talk.

"Well," says one, "pretty good storm last night."

"Yep," says the other, taking off his feed cap and wiping his shockingly white forehead. "You got anything left?"

"Nope," says the first one, "it was pretty much level when I came to Kansas, and now it's pretty much levelled again."

Folks, I'd like to see us adopt these new state symbols. We shouldn't be afraid to let the rest of the world understand Kansas and Kansans. Besides, some day my Grandson will know all the old symbols, and I'd like some new ones so I can stump him next Kansas Day, when we'll be . . . how old?

ANSWERS TO SYMBOLS QUIZ

1. "Ad Astra Per Aspera" means "To the Stars Through Difficulties." Or, the Here, Kansas, translation: "Give Me Another Aspirin."

2. Buffalo.

3. Western Meadowlark.

4. "Home on the Range."

5. Sunflower.

6. "People of the South Wind."

7. "The Kansas March."

8. Solid blue, with a sunflower in the middle.

9. Cottonwood.

10. Sunflower State, Wheat State, Jayhawker State (only we let the University of Kansas steal the meaning from it), or, as I like to call us, "The Fly Swatter State" (more about that later).

11. Honeybee.

12. Ornate box turtle.

13. Barred tiger salamander

14. Harney silt loam

Here, Kansans Know All the Words to "Home On the Range"

The song, Home On The Range, is as truly Kansas as the sunflower & the jayhawk and has grown to such immense popularity that admirers in other states have often tried to change the words to make them applicable to their locality.
—*Laws 1947, Chapter 433*

You're a true Here, Kansan in direct proportion to your recollection of the verses of "Home on the Range." And before you read one more word, you should go off by yourself and write down as much of that song as you can remember.

Now, I'll bet the same thing happened to you that happens in Here, Kansas, where we citizens gather together every 4th of July. We don't call it an Old Settler's Reunion, because everyone in Here is already old, and we live here year round. In fact, it's a reunion of the young and restless: for all our kids and grandkids gone off into the world to find something better than Here, Kansas.

But the 4th is mighty fine. Every resident and visitor joins the Here parade. We have to tie up our dogs along Kansas Street as an audience to parade for. We march in a circle at the end of the street, so the front of the parade can see the back of it. Then we gather for a picnic in the shade of the grain elevator, and wait for nature's sparklers, lightning bugs.

Every year, as evening settles and the air cools to the low nineties, one of the young and restless strums a guitar and announces, "I'll play one we all know." Then we hear, "Oh, give me a home . . ." and a strong first verse: the home and the buffalo, the deer and the antelope, no discouraging words and unclouded skies. And then the chorus. And then nothing.

"Short song," says one of the old folks, and begins another verse. The other old-timers join in. We sing about the bright diamond sand, the glittering streams, the white swan like a maid in a heavenly dream.

Then the chorus, then the gale of the Solomon vale where life streams with buoyancy flow and the banks of the Beaver where no poisonous herbage doth grow.

Most everyone drops out, but Elmer Peterson and Claude Anderson and Mabel Beemer and I sing about the bright heavens, the twinkling stars, how their glory does not exceed that of ours.

Then the verse about the wild flowers, the curlew's scream, the antelope flocks on the hillsides so green.

For the final verse it'll just be Mabel Beemer, in a high, wavering voice, singing of pure air, fine breezes, about how she would not exchange her home here, to range forever in azure so bright.

Her voice falls away, and around us fireflies wink, and above us the sky is shot through with stars. For a moment everything is fine.

"I didn't know there was so many verses," says one of the young folks. "How can you remember them all?"

"Because we're true-blue Kansans," I want to say, but I let his question die.

But there's another reason we remember all of them: For us, they were true. We Kansas old-timers have not exchanged our homes here to range into the bright land of American corporate opportunity. In our early days, deer and antelope played alongside our cattle. The curlews, and the killdeer in buffalo grass, screamed their joy, and meadowlarks whistled like farm kids doing chores. The air was pure, the creeks ran full—at least in the spring—and we didn't have half the noxious weeds farmers spray for these days. The beauty of the wildflowers could still knock your breath away.

Kansans forget the verses of "Home on the Range" because they can't imagine them to be true. But they were. "Home on the Range" was not just the state song, it was the state itself.

Imagine 1873. You are Dr. Brewster Higley. You've left LaPorte, Indiana, and your fifth wife (which might account for the seldomness of discouraging words). You've settled on 160 acres near Smith Center. You wander down to Beaver Creek, hoping to shoot one of the deer and antelope that graze the rich Solomon River Valley. You look around you and are overcome by Kansas, and so you write a poem, "Western Home." The Smith County Pioneer prints it, a local druggist sets it to music, and folks love it. They sing it everywhere, transforming the words to fit Arizona or wherever they roam. President Franklin Roosevelt claims it as his favorite song, and by 1947 it is adopted by your state to represent everyone's feelings about Kansas.

Then imagine a July night surrounded by lightning bugs. You're sitting beside the Here, Kansas, grain elevator, singing. You remember all the verses to "Home on the Range," and not just because it's the state song. You know them because they are the Kansas you believe in again.

HOME ON THE RANGE
(as first printed in the Smith County Pioneer)

Oh give me a home, where the buffalo roam,
Where the deer and the antelope play,
Where seldom is heard, a discouraging word
And the sky is not clouded all day.

Chorus:
A home, a home, where the deer and the antelope play,
Where seldom is heard, a discouraging word
And the sky is not clouded all day.

Oh, give me the gale of the Solomon vale,
Where life streams with buoyancy flow,
On the banks of the Beaver, where seldom if ever
Any poisonous herbage doth grow.

19

Chorus

Oh, give me the land where the bright
    diamond sand
Throws its light from the glittering stream,
Where glideth along the graceful white swan
Like a maid in a heavenly dream.

Chorus

I love the wild flowers in this bright land of ours,
I love, too, the wild curlew's scream,
The hills and white rocks and antelope flocks
That graze on the hillsides so green.

Chorus

How often at night, when the heavens are bright
With the light of the glittering stars,
Have I stood here amazed, and asked as I gazed
If their glory exceeds this of ours.

Chorus

The air is so pure, the breezes so free,
The zephyrs so balmy and light.
I would not exchange my home here to range
Forever in azure so bright.

Here, Kansans Are Proud of Their Town

[In Kansas] so many towns were planned and started that settlers worried lest there be too little land left for farming. The territorial legislature in 1859 passed a resolution stating that every alternate section of land should be set aside for farming.
—John Rydjord,
Kansas Place-Names

In Kansas, almost every little town has a gimmick, something to promote itself, something for passersby to remember, something that brings honor or distinction. I suppose it's boosterism, pure and simple, and it's harmless, in its own way.

Here, Kansas, once became embroiled in boosterism, back when Hattie and Tommy Burns of the Here College of Beauty and Fiberglass Maintenance took a trip to see Kansas. They came back steamed up and called a town meeting. I presided.

"Everywhere you go," said Hattie, "people are proud of where they live." She brought out a sheet of paper. "Fortunately, we took notes."

"Excellent notes," nodded Tommy. And he opened a dog-eared spiral notebook.

Hattie adjusted her trifocals. "I was in charge of what we called our 'World' category." And she began to read. "Topeka has the 'World Famous Zoo.' Greensburg has the 'World's Largest Hand-Dug Well.' Cawker City has the 'World's Largest Ball of Twine,' or maybe second largest, but even the controversy is good for them. And both Burlington and Chetopa claim to be the 'Catfish Capital of the World.' To go with your catfish, we have Lenexa, 'Spinach Capital of the World.' And then there's Dodge City, the 'Cowboy Capital of the World.' And here's a good one, from a town that kept trying until they got it right." Hattie held up her notebook like it was the Statue of Liberty's Torch. "Garden City, the home of the 'World's Largest Free Municipal Concrete Swimming Pool.'"

"Now I found some 'State's largest,'" said Tommy. "Everest is 'Home of the Largest Red Cedar Tree in the State,' and Pretty Prairie is 'Home of the State's Largest Night Rodeo.'" He turned the page. "And there's a 'State's Widest,' too. Plains, Kansas, with 'Kansas' Widest Main Street.' Yep, they have an annual toilet race. Stools on wheels, or something."

"Then there's your honorary Kansas capitals," said Hattie, flipping another page of her notebook. "'Pheasant Capital of Kansas' is Norton. 'Czech Capital of Kansas' is Wilson. 'Pinto Bean Capital of Kansas' is Leoti. Great

Bend is the 'Oil Capital in the Heart of the Wheat Belt.' And Russell Springs is the 'Cow Chip Capital of Kansas.' They even have them a Cow Chip Throwing Contest."

Tommy interrupted her list. "I found what I call the 'Halfways,'" he said proudly. "Luray is 'Halfway Between Paradise and the Garden of Eden.' Kinsley is 'Halfway and a Place to Stay,' being exactly between New York City and San Francisco."

"And there's the 'Firsts,'" Hattie shouted out. "'First Cattle Town in Kansas,' Baxter Springs. 'First Free Public Library in the State,' Peabody."

"And the outlaw towns," Tommy interrupted her again. "Meade practically lives off the Dalton Gang Hideout. Coffeyville took the bank where the Daltons got shot and turned it into a museum. Cherryvale has the Bloody Benders. And Lawrence has Quantrill."

Hattie pushed herself forward. "And Mission and Baldwin City and Council Grove and Pawnee Rock and Larned all have the Santa Fe Trail."

Well, folks, I wasn't sure if the two of them

would ever run out of steam, and I could see by now where they were headed. "So what's Here, Kansas, got?" I asked. "What do you want us to put up a sign for and call ourselves so that we can boost our fine community?"

"We don't know," said Hattie. "That's why we called a meeting. We want a committee."

And you know, this committee was good for us. We researched the town, we learned our history, we learned Kansas. We contacted the State Historical Society, the Kansas Chamber of Commerce, we got all the old folks to talking. And after it was all over, we boosted ourselves as well as we could. Now, in fine paint, weathered only a little by Kansas sun and wind, just outside of Here, is a sign. If you squint, you'll be able to read the tiny letters: "Visit the World's First, Smallest, Brick, South-Facing, Abandoned Carnegie Library in Kansas, From Which the Dalton Gang Checked Out a Guide to Coffeyville, Kansas."

Folks, I'm not sure this sign has increased our tourist traffic, but it sure has given us a little civic pride.

Looking for Here on the map? Here are other towns you won't find:

Reno County once had towns named PURITY and DESIRE;

There was an ECHO in Douglas County;

NOVELTY, in Montgomery County, lasted from May to June of 1881;

ROCK-A-BY survives as ROCK in Cowley County;

TIDY, in Stafford County, might be an EXAMPLE (Haskell County) to HAPHAZARD in Dickinson County;

A town named MIRAGE lasted for 10 years in Rawlins County;

There is no longer any AIR in Lyon County;

YOUNG AMERICA lasted only a few years in Osage County;

GOOD INTENT, later shortened to GOODINTENT, was named by Hattie Dorman when this Atchison County community started a Sunday School;

There was an ECHO again in 1874, in 1878, in 1894, in 1900.

Here and There: Kansas Place Names— a State of Confusion

Folks, you already know that There, Kansas, is the county seat of There County. You can't find it on the map, but it's there. I can't exactly tell you where, because it's not all that easy to get from Here, where I live, to There. It's easy to get to Near Here, though, and by then, you're nearly there, anyway. We're a simple county, somewhere in the middle of what ought to be a simple state. But recently, I've been getting awfully confused.

You see, my great-grandson came for a visit from Topeka. He brought along some homework, part of a social studies unit on Kansas. For extra credit, he was memorizing the Kansas counties and their county seats. He knew I'd help him, as much as I love this great state.

I unfurled my big Kansas map. "Well," I said to him, "let's make it easy. You're in There County. County seat is There. You see: There, There. There's going to be a bunch of them the same. Learn them first."

"Great," he said. He started down the county list, and studied his map. "Atchison," he said, "is county seat of Atchison County."

Meanwhile, I went down the list of cities and towns. "Wait," I said, "don't forget Allen, and Chase, and Chautauqua, and Cherokee, and Ellis. Those are all counties, too."

That's when the confusion began. I'll put it in a nutshell: although 41 Kansas towns share names with a Kansas county, only 24 of those towns are even in the county they share a name with; and of those 24, only 14 of those towns are actually the county seat, like There, Kansas, is to There County. So, you're okay if you want Ellis and Ellis, or Washington and Washington, or Leavenworth and Leavenworth, or Pratt and Pratt. But Ford is not the county seat of Ford County, nor Harper of Harper County, nor Jewell of Jewell County, nor Stafford of Stafford County. And if you want to get even more geographically confused, I'll tell you that Greeley is not in Greeley County, but in Anderson; and Kiowa is not in Kiowa County, but in Barber; and Ottawa is not in Ottawa County, but in Franklin, though you won't find Franklin in Franklin because it's in Crawford County.

"Wait," I said to my great-grandson after I studied the map again, "there's going to be some simple ones like Clay Center, the county seat of Clay County."

He looked at the county names again, and wrote down Coffeyville, Edwardsville, Harveyville and Johnson City. "Are these what you mean?" he asked me, his young face full of hope.

"Let's see," I said, but I should have known. Folks, Coffeyville isn't in Coffey County, it's in Montgomery County, three counties down. Edwardsville is in Wyandotte County, some 300 miles from Edwards County. Harveyville is in Wabaunsee County and Johnson City in Stanton, as far from Johnson County as you can be and still stay in Kansas. One good thing, though: If it says "center," then it truly is the county seat of that same county—Clay Center, Rush Center, Smith Center. I told that to my great-grandson.

"Thanks," he said. But then he took his book and went to another room. I didn't blame him. A confused teacher is worse than no teacher at all. But I can't take all the blame. What about Kansas? If Kansas was a state of mind, I'd call it disoriented.

Later that evening I went to my great-grandson's room. He tried to focus on the Kansas map in front of him. "How're you doing?" I asked him.

"It's hard," he said. "A lot harder than I thought."

I patted him on the back and tried to sympathize. "There, there," I said to him. "There, there."

"Easy for you to say," he said back.

Folks, if you're ever going to travel Kansas, take along your map, study it hard, and don't take anything for granted. Even a Kansas insider can become mighty confused.

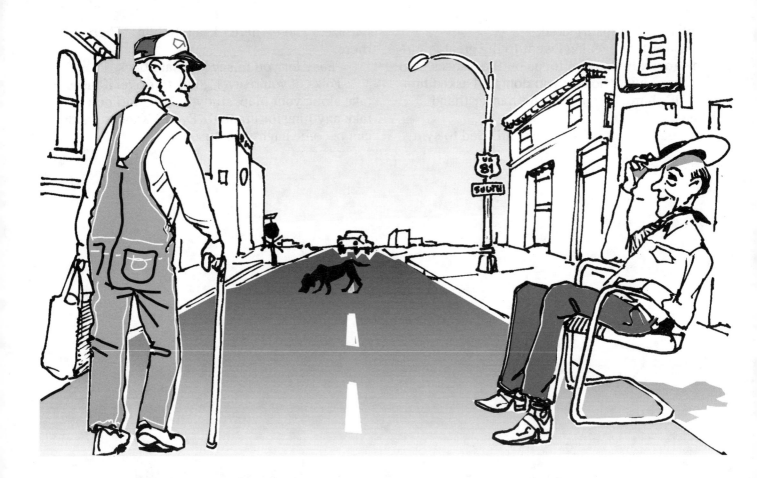

Here, Kansans Live On the Kansas Great Divide

The north side is literary, religious, commercial; the south side possesses the large hotels, the saloons, and the places where dealers in cardboard, bone and ivory congregate. On the north side of the track you are in Kansas, and hear sober and profitable conversation; when you cross to the south side you are in Texas.
—Topeka Record, writing of Abilene, Kansas, August 5, 1871

If you're curious, you're probably wondering: "Where is Here, Kansas?" I'll tell you: real close to Highway 81. Why, I can walk from Elmer Peterson's Drive-Thru Pharmacy and Car Wash at the corner of John Brown and Kansas streets down to the Co-op at the corner of Wyatt Earp and Kansas streets, and feel like I've moved from Eastern to Western Kansas.

You know, U.S. 81 gets blamed for dividing this state, Eastern from Western Kansas. Folks west of Concordia, Salina, McPherson and Wellington are thought by eastern Kansans to be "out there." In fact, one Kansas historian named his book WEST OF WICHITA because he thought the experiences west were so different from those east of Wichita.

Of course, there were divisions long before Highway 81. Geography started it: Prairie to the east, Plains to the west; 33 inches of rainfall to the east, 14 inches to the west; bluestem grass to the east, buffalo grass to the west.

Experience continued it. Eastern Kansas was settled before the Civil War, and the politics of North vs. South were embedded in the Eastern Kansas mind. And what was embedded in the Western Kansas mind? The cattle drive, the sod house, the windmill, barbed wire strung to stone fence posts, buffalo-dung fuel. And wind.

Economics continues it. Suburban Johnson County is not like Johnson, Kansas, though they are both wealthy because of where they are: Johnson County near industrial, service-laden Kansas City; Johnson, Kansas, above the Largest Natural Gas Field in the United States.

Here, Kansas, being near U.S. 81, is full of all these Kansas differences. The eastern half of Here wears overalls, work boots, feed caps, shirts we button to the collar for warmth; we drink water and eat fried chicken; our heroes are John Brown, William Allen White, Dwight David Eisenhower; our women quilt, read from the Bible, and save their egg money.

The western half of Here wears Levi's and pointy-toed cowboy boots, ten-gallon hats, pearl-buttoned shirts open at the collar, with a kerchief at the neck; we drink whiskey and eat bloody steaks; our heroes are Wyatt Earp, the Dalton brothers, and Mike Hayden (who brought Western Kansas speech back to the statehouse); our women drive pickups, throw darts, and know how to dance in high-heeled boots.

The eastern half mutters while the western half curses, each at the other.

You know, in Here, Kansas, we're stronger for our differences. Back in the '40s, Milton Eisenhower wrote a piece he called "The Strength of Kansas." He felt our state's spirit came from the interaction between New England and the South, Puritanism and the Wild West, thus producing what he called "hybrid vigor." He ended by saying the Kansas spirit is a "unique mingling of Puritan morality, Southern Chivalry, and Western individualism." He claimed that "no state is more accurately representative of America as a whole than Kansas." And while we're bragging, let me say this: No town in this state represents Kansas more truly than Here.

So goodbye. I'll see some of you at church, some at the rodeo. And God bless some of you, and the hell with the rest of you.

Here, Kansans Are "True Kansans"

Banger and I have known each other for a very long time. He is worried that living on the East Coast might have rearranged the bone in my head. That's what we say out on the high plains when someone has lost sight of the singular madness that is necessary to get from January blizzards to the May tornadoes, and from there to the August branding irons—all on beans and rice, a little whisky, and no doubt some crooked cigarettes: Don't let the bone in your head get bent. Bent head bones can lead to rounded edges, polished boots, fashionable women and trucks with stereos in them. It is thought you can disappear into such a world and never be seen again as yourself.

—Bob Day,
"Not in Kansas Anymore"

My grandson, Thomas Jefferson Oleander, called me from Topeka the other night: "Gramps, I read something about Kansas you'll want to know. About population. Seems that 67 percent of all Americans live within an hour's drive of a coast."

"What's that got to do with Kansas?" I asked.

"Well, it means Kansans are among the 33 percent of Americans who actually live in America. We're not crowding the East Coast thinking how we came from Europe. Or the West Coast, thinking we've discovered heaven. Or the Florida coast, pretending to be Caribbean. Or the Texas gulf, spicing seafood with Mexican peppers. It means Kansans are true Americans, living on the land, not the sea. Gramps," he concluded, "the farther you get from the salty sea, the more you become the salt of the earth."

"I guess you're right," I said. "How's things in Topeka?"

"Great," he said. "The wife and I drove to Kansas City last weekend. Had a fine time.

Everywhere you turn, they've got a cappuccino bar. You know how I like coffee. Life is improving. You can even buy live lobsters at Topeka supermarkets now."

"Great," I said. "I'll come up and see you real soon. And thanks for the population fact." I hung up.

Folks, Thomas Jefferson Oleander has a point. There is a big heartland of America, with a small population compared to that hour's drive from a coast. Some folks seem to like an ocean of seawater more than an ocean of grass. They prefer forests to open spaces. They want the latest everything more than they want to be the last to get anything—from cappuccino to lobster. They don't want to be Kansans.

You know, in The Wizard of Oz, Dorothy tells the scarecrow all about missing home. He says, "I cannot understand why you should wish to leave this beautiful country and go back to the dry, gray place you call Kansas."

"That is because you have no brains," she tells him. "No matter how dreary and gray our homes are, we people of flesh and blood would rather live there than in any other country, be it ever so beautiful. There is no place like home."

And folks, I'm kind of like Dorothy. I'm proud to live in Kansas, and even prouder to live in Here, Kansas. In fact, if my grandson Thomas Jefferson Oleander claims Kansas as salt-of-the-earth, heartland America, then I'll claim Here, Kansas, as the salt-of-the-earth heart of Kansas. He did it with population statistics, so I will, too.

Grab a Kansas map and draw one sixty-mile circle around Kansas City and another around Wichita. You know how many Kansans live in those circles? Almost 67 percent—same as the number of Americans an hour's drive from the coast. That means 67 percent of Kansans are an hour's drive from a live lobster and a cappuccino bar.

I called Thomas Jefferson. "You're a true American," I said, "but not a true Kansan."

Then I gave him some advice: buy a lobster, put it in a plastic bag of salt water and start west. As soon as someone scratches his head and asks, "What the hell is that?" you'll be in true Kansas, maybe in Here, Kansas. Stop a while and talk to those flesh-and-blood American heartlanders. Talk about grass and wind and sky. About weather and seasons, the extremes of hot and cold. Talk cattle and pigs, catfish and antelope, coyotes and buffalo.

Then ask them how many hours to the nearest coast. Don't be surprised when they tell you. They may be Here, Kansans, but they're Americans, too.

Here, Kansans Vote Like Kansans

Time was, when they used to say in Kansas that the Republican Party and the Methodist church were the spiritual forces that controlled the State.
—William Allen White, "Kansas: A Puritan Survival"

Folks, it used to be easy to vote like a true-blue Kansan. We registered Republican, we voted Republican. We ended up with losers like Alf Landon or winners like Dwight David Eisenhower, but we were happy.

You see, Kansans were intimately involved in the pre-Civil War struggle over slavery. Any good Free-Stater was in the party of Abraham Lincoln. During the war, Kansas enlisted more men per capita for the Union cause than any other state. And Kansas suffered more casualties per capita than any other state after Pennsylvania. So after the war, Kansas was the Free State, the Union State, and the destination for Union veterans taking advantage of the Homestead Act of 1862.

My God, in those days, town after town had its chapter of the G.A.R. (Grand Army of the Republic). Those old veterans took their uniforms out of mothballs every Fourth of July and paraded up and down Kansas Main Streets in a fit of pride, nostalgia and Republican fervency.

I remember that my grandfather and some

of his G.A.R. outfit always put on their uniforms one other time: election day, when they went to the polls. I don't need to tell you how they voted.

Sure, we Kansans have had our quirks. Why, in 1896, times were so hard a majority of Kansans abandoned the true blue of the Republican Union Army. But they didn't vote the gray of the Confederate Democrats. They voted the green of the Populists: green because these folks didn't have much experience in politics; green because they envied the greenback currency that none of them had; green because they had once raised corn and were now raising hell.

So Kansas elected Populist Governor Lorenzo D. Lewelling. One of his campaign promises: He would let anybody in the state come take a bath in the extravagant marble bathroom the Republicans had installed at taxpayer expense in the governor's offices in the Capitol building. Later on, Lewelling stood on the Capitol steps and spotted a flying saucer, the first political UFO sighting in Kansas history.

In 1930, during other hard times, Kansans elected a Democrat by a fluke. What we really wanted was an Independent goat-gland doctor by the name of John Richard Romulus Brinkley, M.D., Ph.D., M.C., D.P.H., Sc.D. Sure, the doctor was under suspicion for medical malpractice: his medical "operation" transplanted a reproductive gland from the Arkansas Toggenberg goat (they don't smell as sharp as other breeds) into the human male, which guaranteed to bring about the "resumption of man's God-given role on this beautiful earth."

And Brinkley owned a 100,000-watt radio station, KFKB (Kansas First, Kansas Best), and a Lockheed airplane. When he filed as an Independent candidate just 42 days before the election, he took to swooping his plane into Kansas fields, disgorging a Methodist preacher, gospel singers, and his own cheerleaders who would teach the crowd to spell his name correctly when they wrote it in on the ballot. He promised to pave Kansas roads, put a lake in every county, and do away with what he called "unnecessary boards and investigative bodies," which everyone knew meant that he was tired of being tried by the Kansas Board of Medical Registration and the Federal Radio Commission. One of his campaign slogans reminded us of Populist days. Brinkley said: "LET'S PASTURE GOATS ON THE STATEHOUSE LAWN."

For that, we gave him 239,000 votes. Some 50,000 of those were declared void by election officials—seems those cheerleaders hadn't worked the crowd hard enough, and any ballot that did not spell Brinkley's name just as he'd filed was invalidated. And thrown away. Why, to this day you'll find Kansans who remember seeing those ballots floating in bales down the Kansas River. The Republican and Democrat vote tallies were so close that in any other year both would have demanded a recount. As it was, with the prospect of a Brinkley challenge breathing down their necks, everyone left well enough alone, and the Democrat, Harry A. Woodring, who later joined F.D.R.'s cabinet, became governor by a margin of just 257 votes.

Recent Kansas voting history shows that you can't just vote Republican and smile any-more, especially not in the governor's race. Why, in the 1990 election, we voted in a woman for the first time. She had been a Republican, but turned Democrat. Then she ran on the rhetoric of Populism. Claimed to represent The People. What she didn't tell everyone was that The. (short for Theodore) People is an old blind man who lives down the street from me in Here, Kansas, and we in Here stopped listening to him long ago.

Yes sir, I believe Governor Joan Finney is living proof that Kansans are true democrats: We will allow anyone to govern us. Lewelling did back in the 1890s. Brinkley would have done it in the 1930s. Joan Finney did it from 1991 to 1995. But none of them shows Kansas voters to be any smarter than they were years ago, when they didn't think at all, just voted true-blue Republican.

So, how does a true Kansan vote these days? Well, we exercise two options. Some of us think as hard as we can, we weigh the issues, listen to the debates, and vote to the very best of our abilities. The rest of us go into the voting booths blindfolded, feel our way randomly through the selections, pull the lever and watch the TV to see what we've done. The results, it seems to me, are about the same.

Here, Kansans Enjoy Their Hypocrisies

It is the quality of piety in Kansas to thank God that you are not as other men are, beer-drinkers, shiftless, habitual lynchers, or even as these Missourians.
—*E.H. Abbott*

No Kansan likes to do anything easy. He raises his crops hard. He takes his religion hard. To be able to get licker [sic] easy would just be contrary to nature for him. So he makes laws to keep him from gettin' it . . . which makes it harder, which give mo' of a point to drinkin' it, an' behold, yo' Kansan thereby derives greater satisfaction of soul out'n it.
—*a Texan explains Kansas liquor laws in Paul I. Wellman's Bowl of Brass*

When you're young, you're always frustrated because things don't change, or, if they do change, they don't change fast enough. When you're old, it's a comfort to you how things stay the same.

I thought of that the other day down at the Here, Kansas, Mini-mart, where I buy my beer and chewing tobacco.

When I was a young man, proper young women had slogans to express their principles. Henrietta Shaw once said to me: "Lips that touch liquor shall never touch mine." Now there was an incentive; you'd agree if you ever saw Henrietta's lips, let alone kissed them. Kansas was legally dry, had been since 1881, and was considered a progressive state. You see, alcohol was a national problem. There was no federal "war against alcohol," but folks united and the nation legislated itself dry in 1919.

Of course that didn't stop folks, myself included, from drinking. I did stop, though, for a month, because of Henrietta's lips. When I lost Henrietta, I lost my incentive. The USA lost its

41

incentive in 1933, and Kansas mostly did in '49, though we've still got more laws than buttons on Henrietta's dress. Nowadays, the schools are full of "Just Say No," and the federal government is suddenly on beer cans, in fine print, like the part of a contract that screws you over. Their warning: Don't drink when you're pregnant; Don't drink when you're driving or operating heavy machinery; and Drinking may cause health problems.

I love that kind of understatement, like when my daddy used to say: "I'd stay out of the north forty; the bull might have woke up on the wrong side of the bed." Folks, bulls don't have any other side of the bed. Alcohol doesn't either. Neither does tobacco. Of course it's bad for you. Anybody knows that who spits a nice drool of brown juice into a cup and tries to look at it without a little turn of the stomach.

I remember my first tobacco warning. Henrietta Shaw said, "I don't smoke, and I don't chew, and I don't go with the folks who do."

Lots of folks chewed. So many that every hotel lobby, hardware store, bank and grocery had a spittoon in the corner.

When was the last time you saw a spittoon, except in your county historical museum? Young Claude Hopkins took the last spittoon in Here out of the Mini-mart years ago. Then, the other day, he took out the ashtrays too. Henrietta would be proud. Not only do you have a smoking section, but you have to ask for an ashtray to stump your butt.

Twenty years from now, some little kid will probably point to an ashtray in a county museum display and say, "Mommy, what's that?"

"An ashtray," the mother will say.

"But what is it for?" the kid will ask.

The mother will explain while the little kid smirks: His mother is crazy to believe anyone would light a fire on a stick of tobacco, suck up the smoke and blow it out, and knock the ashes into a little plastic dish that says "Coors" on it.

But it's true, all of it. And it hasn't changed since I was young. There's a comfort in that. You see, I'm a Here, Kansan. And we Here, Kansans don't like our pleasure if there isn't a little guilt to it. So bless the government for warnings and smoking ordinances, for slogans and for wars against bad habits.

And bless you, Henrietta. I'll blow you a kiss clear back into the past. By the time it reaches you, the smell of alcohol and chewing tobacco will have wafted into the air and disappeared. That kiss will be as pure as the memory of my brief love for you.

Here, Kansans Know How to Test Their Politicians

Every year, a delegation from Here, Kansas, takes a trip to the Kansas State Fair in Hutchinson. We meet our State Representative there to play what we call the Fair Game. Here's how it works: You find your local politicians, you blindfold them, and then you take a quick tour of the Fair. They describe what they're hearing. It's that simple. And though they're blindfolded, it's always an eye opener.

Take a representative we elected a while back. I can't remember if I voted for him. He's a young fellow, been to Here, Kansas, maybe once in his life. His hand, when I shook it, was soft as a satin pillow. He wore a suit he couldn't have bought west of U.S. Highway 81, and pointy shoes you only see on the TV. He brought his own blindfold, the kind Elizabeth Taylor wears so she can sleep between husbands.

Well, we started through the Kansas State Fair. First off, we walked by a middle-aged couple with a bunch of whiney kids. The man was tired; you could hear it in his voice. They were arguing

45

about money, what they could afford, while their kids whirled around screaming.

"I know," piped up State Rep., "that's a political debate, economic policy."

Well, we hadn't moved but two more steps when off in the distance we heard some old guys throwing horseshoes, that beautiful clang of curved iron against steel pole, the thud of weight against clay.

"Let me guess," said State Rep., cocking his head, "that's got to be some legislator putting a flag up a flagpole, showing his patriotism. Don't you love how the metal fasteners hit the flagpole? How the flag sounds in the Kansas wind? Don't you just love everything about the flag? I know I do."

We shoved him along. We hadn't moved but ten feet when some little kid walked by with a balloon. It broke and the kid screamed for another.

"That's some kid blowing up one of those free condoms Planned Parenthood is giving away," said State Rep. "Just what will they expose our children to next?"

I wanted to nip that in the bud, so I said, "Rep., it has writing on it."

He shook his head. "When I was a boy they gave away yardsticks with ads," he said. "Don't tell me they're putting advertising on condoms."

Well, it only got worse for State Rep. from there on. He confused the pig races with the sound of his colleagues lining up for the pension fund. He called the monotonous tone of an auctioneer a Bob Dole stump speech. I guess I don't have to tell you, but our State Rep. heard the darnedest things. Why, when we took him by an old-fashioned milking demonstration, he confused the beautiful sound of streams of milk hitting the bottom of a bucket with the sound of a coffee machine in the Kansas Statehouse.

Finally, we were ready for the long ride back to Here, Kansas. We thanked State Rep. for playing the Fair Game. He turned and looked back on the Kansas State Fair, the buildings full of animals, the food booths, the rides, the rooms full of pies, cakes, crops, quilts, grains, implements, everything that is Kansas. "Whatever else I can say, I know this," said State Rep., "I love this great state of Kansas. And I hope I can count on your votes."

Folks, my hearing isn't real good, but from somewhere deep in the fair I heard one of those great big showcase bulls dump a mighty big load. And, having heard enough B.S. for one day, I clicked my heels and went home knowing who to vote against.

Here, Kansans Grew Tired of Celebrating the Ike Centennial

[Eisenhower] appeared to be, in several respects, the archetypical Kansan. The wide and sunny skies of his state, and the width and openness of the Dickinson County landscape, might be seen in his wide sunny grin, in his seemingly invincibly sunny and open disposition. . . . [His Kansas] boyhood seemed designed in general to promote a psychology of "middleness" or "togetherness" that worked against unequivocal either- or choices and for coalitions, amalgamations, homogenizations on the basis of perceived common denominators among diverse people and things and forces. Such twentieth-century "Kansas" qualities . . . were essentially conservative attributes of a successful "chairman-of-the-board," which is exactly what Eisenhower frankly said he was. A hostile critic might even see them as pernicious insofar as they encouraged halfway measures—measures that were, in effect, affirmations of the status quo—in situations demanding bold decision on the side of change, of novelty.
—Kenneth S. Davis, Kansas: A Bicentennial History

Here, Kansas, was sure glad to blow out the candles on Ike's centennial cake. As for me, I paraded, and I went to conferences, and I listened to radio programs, and watched TV specials. I saw Ike's picture on posters, flyers and in the newspaper so much I dreamed I woke up in the morning bald, a big smile plastered on my face. I even went to see the butter sculpture of Ike and Mamie at the Kansas State Fair in Hutchinson, and somehow it seemed okay: He was kind of the cream of Kansas, the butter on the common loaf most Kansans represent. But butter melts, even gets rancid after a while.

You see, I once liked Ike. I liked him back during W.W. Two, when he got the Allied forces together and pulled off the final stages of the war as Supreme Commander of the European Theater of Operations. I liked his ticker-tape parade, the biggest in our history up until then. I liked his satisfaction in being a Kansan, most evident when he returned to his home town after the New York parade and said, "The proudest

49

thing I can claim is that I'm from Abilene." I liked his NATO command. In fact, I liked him right up to his presidency. After that, though, it was downhill for Ike, and downhill for Kansas.

Sure, he was popular. Sure, he kept smiling. Sure, it was reassuring to watch him play golf as though the country's problems weren't nearly as irritating as a bad lie in a sand trap. Sure, those were good economic times, some of the last years I made any money farming out in Here, Kansas. And sure, Ike brought Kansas some fame: We caught the reflection from the sun that shone on him. Sure enough, for just a while, Ike was Kansas, Kansas was Ike, and the country liked us.

So why don't I like the Eisenhower presidency? Well, Ike made us Kansans well-liked for all the wrong reasons:

For our traditional conservatism, when in fact we have just as many radical traditions. Remember, I'm named for that greatest of all "Popocrats," William Jennings Bryan, who got so much of his support from the Kansas Populists. Ike should have stood against tyranny in govern-ment; he should have stood against Joe McCarthy.

For our unwillingness to rock the boat on issues like civil rights, when in fact we once had a reputation as "Bleeding Kansas" and elected a black man to a state office as far back as the 1880s. Ike should have enforced the laws without being forced into it, as he was at Little Rock.

For our tolerance, our acceptance, our for-giveness, when in fact we have a tradition for taking up the moral hatchet and slamming it into hypocrisy and lies. Ike should never have embraced Richard Nixon after that B.S. Checkers speech.

By 1961, after eight years of golfing and waf-fling, Ike was history, just like Kansas was histo-ry. There would be a "New Frontier," and a pull away from Ike and the old frontier Kansas repre-sented.

So, when we spent a year celebrating the Eisenhower legacy, we found a lot of good things. So be it. But the close examination of his life and his presidency showed other things, too. One of those is the legacy he left for the Republican presidents who followed him, and what they learned from him: Nixon, to tape his dealings with his staff; Reagan, to smile while the business community runs the White House; and Bush, to keep on golfing even when the country is in one of the biggest sand traps of its history, both economically and in the Persian Gulf, where the world seems "so damn insane" to the rest of us. Oh, Ike, there's times when a good heart and a nice smile just aren't enough. Not even for a Kansan.

Here, Kansans Are Proud of Women in Politics—If They Bring Along Their Harps

Don't tell me you've never heard of Clarina I.H. Nichols, the mother of women's rights in Kansas. She was a newspaperwoman, an early leader in the feminist movement, a friend to Susan B. Anthony and Elizabeth Cady Stanton, and a knitter. And she chose to come to Kansas in 1854.

Now on the surface, you might think she chose Kansas simply as a good place to do her knitting. Because she sat through every session of the Kansas Constitutional Convention, needles in hand, doing her woman's work so that the men attending the proceedings might not be so threatened by the real work she was doing for women. Clarina Nichols listened, lectured, lobbied and labored to see that women were represented in the constitution of the state that would become Kansas.

She is credited with the incorporation of some early constitutional rights for women: liberal property rights, equal guardianship of children, and the right to vote in all school district elections. Bet a lot of the men at the constitutional convention went home knitting their brows, not even a sweater or a scarf to show for their efforts.

When Kansans extended suffrage for women, granting them the right to vote in municipal elections, another Kansas woman made history. I'm sure you've heard of Susanna Madora "Dora" Salter of Argonia, Kansas. She was just 27 years old in 1887, the year some local wags, making fun of woman suffrage and the Women's Christian Temperance Union, put Dora's name on the ballot for mayor. On election day, Ms. Salter was elbows-deep in washing when people came by to tell her she was on the ticket. She promised to serve if elected, and she was and she did, becoming the first woman mayor in the United States on April 4, 1887. She served for a year, earning $1, with very little business: She forced two draymen to buy licenses and she warned some boys about throwing rocks at vacant houses.

But if Susanna Madora Salter didn't go right from cleaning her wash to cleaning up her town, other women did. By 1888, Oskaloosa elected not only a woman mayor, but a full council of women, the first time in history an entire city government was turned over to women. A local newspaper headline read: HOW WOMEN LOSE SELF RESPECT—ARGONIA, SYRACUSE AND OSKALOOSA UNDER FEMALE GOVERNMENT. Another newspaper complained: "There is reason to believe that billiards will soon become a lost art in all the smaller towns of Kansas, for the women have entered politics for the purpose of reforming men." In 1899, President William McKinley said in a public address that Kansas had elected more women to public positions than any other state in the Union, and by 1900 there were 15 Kansas towns with woman mayors.

So what might be a good symbol for women's rights in Kansas? A pair of knitting needles? A wash tub? A broken billiard cue? How about a harp? Joan Finney, the first woman ever elected to be Governor of Kansas, often played the harp at public events. Like her predecessors, she understood that Kansans tolerate women best when their power is tempered by domestication.

So beware the female legislator who does not have a husband, children, a domestic art, dishpan hands, or an attitude about billiards.

Women who want power in Kansas learn to take along a harp.

Here, Kansans Have Their Own Language

Kansas language: directness, bluntness, simplicity of speech, with an admixture of homely and often exceedingly effective humor.
  —Nelson Antrim Crawford, "A Note on the Kansas Language"

Well, I visited my granddaughter, the Kansas City schoolteacher. She's ready for another year of fourth graders. She drove me to a big brick building where each classroom was a sight bigger than the one-room Here School. And a bit prettier, too. I went to school in a stiff white building, wood stove and water bucket in the back, raised platform with the teacher's desk in the front. Our desks marched in straight lines: little desks in front, for the fidgety primary students; big desks in the back—but no matter how big, they were some of them too small for the farm boys who were nothing but overalls, elbows and knees. Our walls were decorated with a map of the United States, a map of Kansas, and a picture of George Washington.

In my granddaughter's classroom, the chairs are blue and orange, and she puts green tennis balls on the bottoms of the chair legs so they don't scrape so loud against the floor. Everywhere you look, there's a poster: a cat hanging at the end of a rope, with the caption, "When you're at the end of your rope, hang in there."

Folks, when I was reading at the fourth level, we had to hang in there or be hung. School was neither colorful nor fun. I remember Miss Lanahan. She never moved from behind her huge desk. If anyone talked out of turn, or moved unnecessarily, or spoke an incorrect answer, she had only to pick up the heavy ruler that lay ready next to her right hand, and the classroom paused and worried about what might happen next. Still, she wanted us to do well, even praised us when we did, though it was a Here, Kansan's sparing praise.

I laughed when my granddaughter showed me the stickers she bought at the school supply. In wild colors, with rainbows, hearts and flowers, those stickers praise and encourage students with the words: Super! Wonderful! Excellent! Fantastic! Great! A+!

Miss Lanahan's encouragement was in Here, Kansas, code, which I'd like to pass along to any of you who have been raised by Here, Kansans, schooled by them, or worked with them. Here, Kansans are not so quick to praise, and when they do, they do it in quiet language. Here's a quick guide to Here, Kansas, praise.

Here, Kansan says:	Here, Kansan means:
"That's not half bad."	"Good."
"Okay."	"Great."
"Pretty good."	"Fantastic."

"Pretty darn good." has no translation—it's extravagant praise. Here, Kansans praise in metaphors, too. Miss Lanahan made us figure out what she meant. Once, my exam was "Cream—with a little work, could be butter." My report was "Almost ready to harvest." Best of all, my overall performance that year was "Sturdy as a German barn." I didn't know it then, but I do now: I got a pretty darn good education from Miss Lanahan.

But Miss Lanahan also taught me to be sparing. As much as I liked my granddaughter's classroom, when she asked what I thought, I said, "It's all right, I guess."

She looked worried for a moment.

"I expect you're a pretty darn good teacher, too," I added. "A real Lanahan."

Then she beamed with pride and thanked me for the compliment. You see, she's used to this old Here, Kansan, and his sparing praise.

Here, Kansans Aren't Afraid To Sound Like Kansans

A writer in Science says that Kansas should be pronounced 'Kansaw.' 'Kansas,' it says, is the French spelling, and the 's' should be silent. Science may be right, but it will be a hard day on the banana industry in Kansas when its people tolerate or sanction any French foolishness in connection with the name of this state. Plain 'Kansas' was good enough for Jim Lane and old John Brown and 'Kansas' it will remain. Don't forget it.
—Harper Sentinel,
February 11, 1888

O
ur state song names Kansas as the place where "Never is heard a discouraging word." But recently, wherever I go, I hear plenty of words to discourage me.

For example, I heard a talk by a celebrated Kansas writer, and every time he mentioned the Arkansas River he pronounced it Arkansaw, like it belonged in that little Southern state that President Bill Clinton comes from. And Kansans these days don't know how to say Osawatomie. They say Ah-sawatomie, as though they don't know the town formed its name by combining the words Osage (from the Osage River) and Pottawatomie (the Indian name). And even my great-grandson goes through Admire on the way to Emporia from Topeka, only he talks as though he admires it. Folks, say "I admire Admire" ten times.

Now, I'm not discouraged only by bad pronunciation. Arkansaw, and Admire, and Ah-sawatomie are just warning signs: They tell us we're losing our identity. Back in 1912, William Allen White wrote about the character of

61

Kansans. He mentioned our "talk," our "something of sprightly picturesqueness of speech. Not everyone can talk the Kansas language," he wrote. "It is an accomplishment. There is no dialect in it—especially—it is a form of imaginative poetic hyperbole. It is full of short cuts to meanings. Single words speak paragraphs."

How we speak has three components. There's pronunciation, of course. And there's what White calls "sprightly picturesqueness." And, finally, there's how we sound: our tone. Some of you will remember a former governor with a nasal voice. Everywhere I went, people were either proud or ashamed of that voice. Even old Claude Anderson, down at the Co-op, would pinch his nose and imitate Mike Hayden. I suspect the state wouldn't have been so darn sensitive unless we knew that Mike Hayden spoke, literally, for Kansans.

Back in 1944, one of our great writers, Joseph Stanley Pennell, reviled that same voice. Of Kansans, he wrote: "They all talked in the same Goddamned flat, nasal voice about the same Goddamned trivial things day-in-day-out year-after-year—eating, sleeping and growing more rustic and pompous and proverbial." Folks, there's some truth in what Pennell wrote about the Kansas voice.

But back to William Allen White. We do have writers who can say much in few words, who create "sprightly picturesqueness." I think of William Stafford, who said so much about Kansas in so few words. Here's a stanza from his poem "Religion Back Home":

The minister smoked,
and he drank,
and there was that woman in the choir,
but what really finished him—
he wore spats.

That "spats" says it all: quietly, humorously, but with finality.

Quietness used to be part of our language. We did not exaggerate in our praise nor in our self-pity. You might know that Kansas suffered a grasshopper invasion in 1874. Even railroads stopped running because the hoppers were so thick the trains couldn't stop once they started—

crushed insects slicked the tracks, you see. During this crisis, one Kansas newspaper editor mentioned the insects only once in his newspaper, and with the short phrase: "A grasshopper was seen on the court house steps this morning."

Folks, let's take off our spats and crank our noses up a few octaves. Here's how William Stafford said it, like a Kansan: "Mine was a Midwestern home—you can keep your world." Keep your world, but remember how to pronounce your home. I'd admire that.

Here, Kansans Don't Like Flashy Things

My husband was a farmer. But he could see beauty in the land. He could see the promise of the seed. Now he was no literary man, but he could almost make a poem out of a clod of dirt.
—Flosse Curtis, Manhattan, Kansas

Claude Anderson walked into the Here, Kansas, Co-op full of pride and uncharacteristic excitement. "My truck's idling, William," he said. "Come on out to my grandson's place and see the latest in tractors."

I got into the truck. "Which grandson?" I asked. "You talking about the one that nearly went bankrupt last year? Or the one who couldn't get into his fields last spring because of the mud? Or the one who lost half the value of his wheat to high moisture content last summer?"

"All three," Claude said. "They went in together and bought a John Deere for all of them to use."

Folks, we drove out from Here, down into southwest There County. The old osage orange trees had littered the ground with yellow leaves and rotting hedge apples. Every farmstead had at least one old oak or maple shimmering orange in the early morning light. Jack O'Lanterns, their carved faces collapsing, tried to keep smiling on farmhouse porches. Everything was just how I like it in the fall: orange, rusting, nestling into the earth for the winter.

Claude and I arrived at his grandson's place, the farm with the double mortgage. The boy led us behind the barn to see that huge tractor, ten-foot tires, enclosed cab, a drive shaft the size of a man. But I was struck most by the colors: bright green, bright yellow. Like Iowa corn before it's ripe, when immature kernels glow yellow and green stalks match the fertilized lawns of suburbia. Corn is full of promise, then.

But corn that looks like John Deere farm machinery is worthless. It's colorful, but it has to survive July insects, August heat, September molds, and the chance of October rains. When the stalks die a pale death, when the ears droop, when the kernels are as hard as an old man's toenail and as orange as the harvest moon—only then do you know what it's worth.

Folks, when I was farming, I always liked Allis-Chalmers machinery. It was orange, like fall itself, the season when farmers look back on their hardships and rewards, when they sit in front of the orange flames of a first fire in the wood stove, to read the smoke of what was for the signs of what will be.

Maybe I'm just an old man, but the spring-time hope that a John Deere machine wants to represent is false. It lies like you lie every spring when you go to the bank and ask for another loan. It lies like you lie to yourself on the way to the elevator, before your crop is weighed, before the price of corn, or wheat, or sorghum falls faster than the temperature in winter.

Sure, farmers ought to have hope. In fact, farmers may be the only optimists left in these United States. But it's age, and longevity, and how things look in the fall that really matters. That's when you look back on the season, or back on your life, and see things for what they are.

"So what do you think?" asked Claude Anderson.

I hoped that Claude's grandsons could survive this new bank loan. I wished the tractor was orange, that these boys could trade the hope of spring for the wisdom of fall. I hoped farming might survive. I had to speak, but I didn't want to offend anyone.

"Pretty green," I said. "It's pretty darn green."

Here, Kansans Hate Wal-Mart

This is America—a town of a few thousand, in a region of wheat and corn and dairies and little groves.
Main Street is the climax of civilization. That this Ford car might stand in front of the Bon Ton Store, Hannibal invaded Rome and Erasmus wrote in Oxford cloisters.

—*Sinclair Lewis,*
Main Street

When Sam Walton died, a lot of merchants in There, Kansas, the county seat of There County, were quietly happy. I don't blame them; they didn't like Sam Walton and his Wal-Marts.

You see, There, Kansas, used to be like a lot of little county seat towns: not booming, not busting. On Main Street you could buy overalls and some white socks at Pete Peacock's clothing store, which we forgave him for calling Peacock's Plumage. Next door, you could buy a hammer, an ax handle, or screws in bulk at Gridley's Hardware. Matt Henry's Appliance Store had everything from toasters to TVs, vacuums to VCRs. If you needed bedsheets, towels, curtains, a kitchen table or a La-Z-Boy reclining chair, you went to Frank Hadtke's Home Furnishings. You get the picture: You could find pretty near everything you might want and stay well within sight of the courthouse; you could do it on the same day you paid your truck tax and registration; and you could still have time for coffee at the Do Drop Inn, where the town merchants congregated when they weren't busy selling to each other.

I liked There, Kansas. Sure, there wasn't much variety in what you could buy. And Matt Henry was slow in deciding to stock VCRs and these home computers. But he'd resisted selling televisions until 1963, when Ruby shot Oswald and people told Matt to stock TVs or they'd find them in Wichita. And the local prices were steep. And you had to wander up and down Main in the cold winter or the hot summer, writing eight different checks, one for each store.

Sam Walton and Wal-Mart changed all that. He built out on the edge of There, along the highway. Sam visited There on the opening day, and he might have been a There County farmer, driving his beat-up old pickup, wearing a feed cap. A lot of people looked at him, grinned, shook his hand or waved. There Countians thought Wal-Mart would be good for There.

They were wrong.

They didn't hear the new employees, mostly busted-out, small-time farmers and their wives, plus some young people still in pimples, all of them in the back, listening to Sam Walton's pep talk and chanting: "Stack it deep, sell it cheap, stack it high and watch it fly! Hear those downtown merchants cry!"

Well, folks, cry they did. Within a year, There, Kansas, had no downtown but the courthouse. Matt Henry sold at a loss, and pulled his two boys out of college. Frank Hadtke closed his family business and took one last La-Z-Boy home, where he's been sitting ever since. Gridley, at the hardware, went from selling screws in bulk to getting screwed by Wal-Mart's bulk buying and selling. When the Do Drop Inn closed, some town wag changed the sign to Don't Drop Inn, which could very well have been the motto for downtown There.

When he died, Sam Walton left behind 23 billion dollars, made off of nearly 2,000 stores. That's about $11,500,000 per store. Unfortunately, although There County consumers saved money, everyone's dollars left There. Every penny saved was stolen from a local pocket to enrich Sam Walton, who saved the local consumer by destroying the local economy. Sam helped make every little Kansas town look alike. Folks, you can say it like a poem, like a chant, like Sam Walton might say it: "Wal-Mart, Pizza Hut, Dairy Queen/ and use the Automatic Bank Card Machine."

You know, if Here, Kansans had any say, we'd make Sam Walton's family create a small-town trust fund with at least half their inherited money. Since Sam took away so much, some of his fortune could go toward reviving the small-town life he destroyed.

The only other solution is simple. Do what Here, Kansans do: Quit buying Wal-Mart; spend more locally and boost your local merchants, your small towns. Think less about quantity and pennies and more about quality and dollars. Think of the little extra you spend as a tax to save whatever little town you might still have left.

Here, Kansans Take Care of Each Other

... Kansans, their character, and their life style are ... decent, caring, friendly, solid, low-key, and independent.
—Robert Smith Bader, Hayseeds, Moralizers and Methodists

Even in Here, Kansas, August is the month of vacations. We like to visit our grandchildren and great-grandchildren when they're not in school. And not many of us farm anymore, so we can always leave our gardens and the few stray animals—dogs, cats, a horse or a cow, some goats or chickens—to a neighbor. In fact, most of us leave our places to Wilbur Schlingensiepen, who likes nothing better than to help us out. Why, some people in Here have even been known to take advantage of Wilbur.

You see, Wilbur's of German heritage, likes everything shipshape, as neat as a pin, in apple pie order. He's a bachelor who spent his life with a spotless mother. He's the kind of man who will clean the grill of his car after every trip to town. He hoes in his garden every day whether or not there are weeds. He shines his boots both before and after he attends the First There Lutheran Church. He'll make puzzle pieces to replace lost ones before he puts the box into the attic, where it will be long after he's gone. In short, he's the kind of man you like to have watching over your place.

Why, I remember last August, when the Lathams left for two weeks. Wilbur was to pick up their mail, feed their goats, and harvest anything from the garden that might otherwise go to the birds, the bugs, or the ground. "Of course," said Wilbur. "Please, don't worry."

The Lathams didn't need to. Why, the first day, Wilbur came into town with the Latham mailbox over his shoulder. "You see," he told us, "the flag is broken off. How do they let the carrier know when they have mail to go out?" He bought a piece of steel, cut it to the correct size, painted it red, and attached it where the old one had been.

The next day, he came into the Co-op with a ten-gallon bucket the Lathams use to feed their chickens. "You see?" he asked, holding it up to the light. "A little hole. First a little hole, then a big one." He bought a new bucket to use while he soldered the old one.

The day after that, he brought in the plastic dishpan the Lathams fill with oats to feed their goats. "Such dirt," said Wilbur. "Even animals, you can't expect them to clean their plates if they do not start with a clean plate." He bought a metal tub, to match the galvanized bucket he'd bought the day before.

The next day, he was in buying screen and staples to repair the Lathams back screen door. "Little holes," said Wilbur, "but big enough for the little bugs."

The day after that he spent repairing the hinges on the Latham's gate. And on it went, for the whole two weeks the Lathams were on vacation.

When the Lathams finally returned, they were amazed. I talked to Charlie Latham down at the Co-op. "No kidding," he said, "Wilbur didn't take any vegetables home, but he canned four quarts of tomatoes, two quarts of beans, and pickled up some okra. You should see the labels he put on the Mason jars!"

But that wasn't all. After Margaret got on the phone, everyone knew everything. Not only did Wilbur bring in the mail, but he sorted it into junk mail, personal mail, and bills. Not only did he bring in the paper, but he circled items in the There County Tattler that he thought the

Lathams might overlook in their haste to catch up on the news.

You know, folks, it turned out the only thing he took was one slice of watermelon. The Lathams found a note taped to the refrigerator, which, by the way, Wilbur had cleaned spotless.

The note read: "The watermelon needs eaten."

Since then, Wilbur has been the housesitter of choice. Here, Kansans might not have an excuse to leave town, but they'll make something up. Because nothing beats the kind of spring cleaning that Wilbur does in the middle of August.

Here, Kansans Like Extreme Weather and Natural Disasters

Carl Becker was a great historian. But then so are most of the old-timers in Here, Kansas.

I walked into the Co-op the other day, and said to Claude Anderson, "My Topeka grandson tells me they've just finished the wettest May since 1892. Had 11.82 inches of rain. Ain't that something?"

"It's something for Topeka," said Claude Anderson. "But don't you go forgetting 1993. You remember when No-mile Creek swole up and my pigs floated all the way to Near Here before they climbed up onto Fred Pete's shed roof?"

"Speaking of roofs," said Barney Barnhill, "why, my great granddaddy used to tell the story of the wettest year in Here, 1877. Back then, everybody lived in a dugout, and God, those sod roofs could leak! Pans all over the tables, chairs and floors to catch the waterfall. And then the Texas cattle came through in that last cattle drive to Hays. They stampeded, and ran right on top of half the dugouts. When they fell through those roofs, folks wondered how it could rain cattle. Yes, sir, there was a beef cow in every pot that year!"

"Beef in a pot is better than grasshoppers in a well," said Elmer Peterson. "My great-grand-mother used to tell us about the Grasshopper Invasion of 1874. Grasshoppers everywhere: ate Kansas all the way to the ground, chewed on the curtains for dessert. Course they fell into the well, then drowned and rotted. 'We drank our coffee awful black that year. Or mostly awful,' my great-grandmother liked to say."

"At least she had coffee," said Mabel Beemer. "Why, during the Dirty Thirties, when we were poor as church mice and twice as rever-ent, we stirred dust into water and called it cof-fee. My poor husband, who loved sugar with his cup, used to smack his dirty lips and say, 'There's nothing sweeter than the Kansas soil.'"

"That's not what they said in Missouri, or Illinois, or Ohio," said Claude Anderson. "I figure they still owe us tons of good topsoil. Ought to give us a rebate on the Illinois corn we buy to feed our cattle."

"At least you've got cattle to feed," said Hattie Burns. "Why, I remember my Great Uncle Robert talking about the blizzard of 1886. Kansas cattle drifted to the fence lines, huddled togeth-er and froze to death. Robert had to burn all the furniture in his house to stay warm. Half the wood floor went, too, before they could get out-side. Lord, we Kansans have seen hard times."

Folks, I went home, and called my Topeka grandson. "So you've had a little rain," I said. And I told him the Co-op catalogue of Kansas disasters.

"Sorry I mentioned it," said my grandson.

"Don't worry about it," I said. "Just keep it in mind. This wet May will be something to talk about. That is, if you can wait 50 years or so."

Here, Kansans Like It Hot

Three thousand days of Kansas sun,
And it comes on again: the six
*   o'clock*
and steel perimeter
upturns beyond the sums and
*   squares*
of window sash, and runs
along the asphalt shingles
of a roof curling
into coral conflagration,
the air between us burning,
burning into day.
*   —Bruce Cutler,*
*   Sun City*

One morning I woke up to a completely still morning in Here, Kansas. No birds, no insects, no wind brushing the curtains through the screened windows, no cars driving by on Kansas Street. I got up and called my friend Mabel Beemer.

"Listen," I said to her, "what do you hear outdoors?"

"Heat," she said. "When it's this hot, things are still. When it stays still, you know it's 'still hot.'"

"Well, let's not stay still," I said.

"Again this year?" she asked.

"Yep," I said. "Everyone else in Here is off driving the roads, enjoying the excitement of wheat harvest."

"And you really want to go out in this heat?" asked Mabel.

Folks, Mabel and I feel different about heat. We feel different in the heat. You see, her circulation is better than mine. From what she tells me, she actually gets hot when the temperature says it's above ninety. I just get comfortable.

I tell you, there's nobody loves the good, dry heat of Central and Western Kansas better than a thin old Kansas man. Ten months of the year my bones ache. I sit shivering on a sunny porch all through spring. I have to stomp my feet to keep my toes from going numb. I turn on my stove burners, hold my hands over them and watch my fingernails turn from blue to pink.

But in July and August I'm finally warm. I'm a snake on a hot rock, a lizard in the desert, ripened wheat waiting to turn gold.

"Thank God for the heat," I told Mabel. "Heat and wheat go together."

"I know heat is part of living in the state of Kansas," said Mabel, "but that doesn't mean we have to celebrate it."

"Celebrating heat is the same as celebrating wheat, and Western Kansas," I told her. "Why, don't you remember the joke Claude Anderson tells us every year, down at the Co-op? The one about the three Kansas boys, all grown up, but only one of them still living in Kansas, still a farmer, the others off in Colorado and California. In their old age they decide to be cremated together. After half a day in the oven, the Californian is burnt to a crisp. In eight hours there's nothing left of the Coloradan. But on the third day, when the oven door is opened, the Kansan sits up and stretches. 'Another day of this good heat,' he says, 'and we'll harvest the wheat.'"

"It'd probably take more than three days to burn you up," said Mabel.

"And you won't burn up in a single day," I said. "Let's take a drive."

We drove around Northwest Kansas, where in three or four days they can bring in more than four million bushels of wheat. Every other vehicle on the road was a grain truck heading to an elevator or railroad siding to sit behind twelve others, waiting to weigh in, dump, and hurry back to the field. Every other field was wheat: cut, being cut, waiting to be cut. The combines—green, red, orange, blue—created billows of chaff. Sometimes baled stubble littered the fields. Some stubble would be plowed under. Some was being burned: five-foot flames licking through the fields.

Folks, it was dusty, and smoky, and the miles seemed to go on forever—miles of wheat, miles of road. But it was beautiful. It was Kansas. And best of all, it was warm.

"Hot!" said Mabel, over and over, as she fanned air from the open window of my 1962 International Harvester truck.

"Hot!" I said back, a big grin on my pink face.

Here, Kansans Don't Believe In Arbor Day

Spring:
Henry dug up a wagonload of seedlings down by the river, and he and Rosie spend several days planting a big grove of cotton-woods along the north side of the claim. ... Rosie conjured up splen-did visions of shade ... as she dug in the soft, mellow ground, and poured buckets of water around the new plants. Every tree would help, too, to bring the change in climate which all of the settlers looked forward to.

Summer, after the grasshopper invasion:
The little cottonwood trees that they had planted in the spring were stripped bare of all leaves, and even the bark was etched in places.

—John Ise, Sod and Stubble

I don't know if you folks remember it, but I do, because it was right on the front page of the paper one Arbor Day, the last time during the Bush administration that the President and his thousand points of light came out to the Great Plains. He was smiling, his foot propped on a shovel, digging a hole to plant a tree. He told us all to do the same. Seems like planting trees will change the face of our Earth. Seems like there's nothing that will fight pollution quicker. Seems like trees are going to save us all, at least that's what George Bush said one Arbor Day. You know, it's such a simple solution I was darn surprised nobody thought of it before.

I quick hopped in my car and headed straight to the Near Here Tavern and Mini-skirt Museum to buy me a money order so I could send away for a tree to plant. But I got side-tracked. Found myself driving down the old dirt road along the east edge of one of my daddy's claims. You know, back in 1873, Congress passed a Timber Culture Act. Settlers could claim a hun-dred and sixty acres if they would plant and maintain some of it in trees, for eight years. My daddy filed. Daddy planted cottonwood, figuring they'd be easiest to grow. He cut sprouts from the river valley and hauled them up to Here. He planted, and watered, and most of them leafed out fine. Then, in 1874, the grasshoppers ate every last one of them down to the ground.

He tried again: hauled, dug, planted, watered. He slaved eight years, breaking his back pumping water, nursing trees through drought, insects, diseases. When he finally proved up on that timber claim, he left the trees on their own. So here I was, driving next to his timber claim, where he planted over a thousand trees (over a thousand points of light, to say it like George Bush might). You know something? Not one tree was left. They were gone by the time I was born, ninety-some years ago. To tell the truth, I saw my first tree when I was six years old, and it was darn frightening.

Still, I drove on toward Near Here, determined to buy a tree, no matter what it cost.

You see, I know how to plant trees. Back in the first part of this century, I helped plant the Kansas National Forest in the Sand Hills along the Arkansas River. The U.S. Government, in all its wisdom, noticed the lack of rainfall on the Great Plains. They had also noticed the absence of trees. Where there were trees, there was rainfall. It didn't take them long to figure that the main thing missing in the Western States was trees. They set aside millions of acres all over the Plains, and started planting trees.

We dug holes and stuck thousands of four-foot pine trees into the good Kansas sand hills. Had to root out some grasses and wild plum just to make room for civilization. I went home after it was all over and waited for rain. I even thought about investing in a nearby galoshes company. Luckily, I kept my hands out of my wallet. You see, after ten years, all that was left of the Kansas National Forest was a bunch of four-foot pine trees, brown and withered, refusing to grow, giving up to grass and plum.

Well, by the time I pulled into Near Here, I had decided to spend my money on beer. As for the tree George Bush planted in South Dakota, somebody's going to have to water it every day. I

84

don't know where they get their water up there. I've walked along the Arkansas River near Garden City and seen how the old cottonwoods on the banks have died, the water table sunk far below their roots. They look like old bones, as old and dusty as George Bush's talk about trees, how they'll change the climate, counteract pollution, save us if we'll save them. Reminds me of that old poem: "I thought that I would never see/ So darn much bull about a tree."

On Kansas

Here, Kansans Used to Say "It Happens First In Kansas"

Kansas is the Mother Shipton, the Madame Thebes, the Witch of Endor, and the low barometer of the nation. When anything is going to happen in this country, it happens first in Kansas. Abolition, Prohibition, Populism, the Bull Moose, the exit of the roller towel, the appearance of the bank guarantee, the blue sky law, the adjudication of industrial dispute as distinguished from the arbitration of industrial differences—these things come popping out of Kansas like bats out of hell.
—William Allen White, 1922

Every Kansas Day, January 29th, I take a little pride in the state. I wake up and read my meditation for the day, a short quote from William Allen White. The one that starts with: "Kansas is the Mother Shipton, the Madame Thebes, the Witch of Endor, ... " and so on.

Now some folks might guffaw at such a proclamation, but not me. If you want to know how Kansas changed the world, you don't have to think any farther than Samuel J. Crumbine, of the State Board of Health. In the first two decades of this century, he helped the world understand infectious disease. White mentioned the roller towel, that monstrosity of dirt and disease whereby germs and grime were recycled person to person in public washing places.

But here's some other things you can thank Crumbine for:

He successfully lobbied hotels for the daily changing of bed sheets, so you don't have to share sheets with whoever had the room the night before you did.

And when you bend over and turn a handle

at a water fountain you can thank Dr. Crumbine for the disappearance of the common drinking cup, which often hung on a dirty string next to a water source, available for dipping water out and dipping germs back in.

And thanks for the knowledge that rats spread diseases.

And thanks for going after the disease-carrying mosquitoes breeding in the potholes of city streets and the mudholes of country lanes.

And then there's the common housefly. Why, back in the nineteenth century, a children's primer might have the letter "F" followed by a verse that read: "Little Fly, Come Sup With Me." It would show a fly sharing a bowl of soup. Crumbine started a national campaign against the fly.

Now, some of you might not believe all this. You might be ready to spit on the sidewalk and say, "That's hard to swallow." Well, just keep your spit in your mouth. Obviously you've not heard how Samuel J. Crumbine proved that spit spreads diseases, too.

But Crumbine wasn't just right, he was good

at educational campaigns. With rats, it was "Bat the Rat." With flies it was "Swat the Fly." Crumbine's "Swat the Fly" took such hold in Kansas that Frank Rose and his Weir City Boy Scout troop took a break from screening windows in Weir: They nailed a square of screen to a ruler, and thus invented the first fly swatter. And the spitting campaign led a Topeka brick manufacturer to produce 100,000 bricks to be laid in the sidewalks, each brick reading "Don't Spit on Sidewalk."

Crumbine met his match during World War I, when he threatened to quarantine Kansas City in the biggest public health crisis of his administration. He wanted to protect Kansans, especially the good soldiers stationed at Fort Riley, from Missouri prostitutes infected with syphilis. He battled with none other than Boss Pendergast, and won. Later, Crumbine outfitted a pullman car to tour the state educating people about sexually transmitted diseases. The legislature promptly cut Crumbine's budget, and he was asked to resign. William Allen White lamented his loss, as all of us should, writing:

"No matter how highly a man may distinguish himself for efficiency and devotion to the public service, he must expect attacks from pin-head politicians who want to attract a little attention. Crumbine has done more for the good fame of Kansas than all the one-horse politicians the state ever grew."

So next time you hear that whenever something's going to happen, it'll happen first in Kansas, for God's sake hold back your spit. Just celebrate how Kansas has changed the world, and thank the Lord you're a Kansan, from "The Fly Swatter State."

Here, Kansans Aren't Sure About Public Art

One of the longest-running debates in the arena of public morality—and the source of much merriment— involves the proper adornment of the capitol dome.

...

The debate continues sporadically to this day, while the dome remains conspicuously unadorned.

—Robert Smith Bader,
Hayseeds, Methodists and Moralists

I've told you I'm old, so it won't surprise you one bit to hear me talk about coins—old coins. If I'd saved just one each of the coins of my youth, I'd have something besides memories to help me through life. But I've got some good memories, and the good thing about memories is when things keep reminding you of them. Take the other day, for example:

I was at the Kansas Statehouse, that monument to just how green copper can get over time. I can remember when that dome blazed in the sun like there might actually be hope for Kansas. Back in those first days, we had big plans for the very tiptop of the building. We were all set to cast a statue of Ceres or Demeter, one of those topless women who dispenses grain, and stick it up there for everyone to see. After all, Nebraska had done it, and neither the Good Lord nor the Ladies' Aid had struck them down. But then the good decent folks of Kansas—we've still got them thicker than smoke in a Bingo parlor—objected. They weren't going to have a heathen woman with breasts showing up there where everyone could see her. It'd be disobeying one of the Ten Commandments, the one about graven images. So we've had us a topless—that is, statueless—dull green statehouse ever since.

Now, like I said, I was in the Capitol the other day. And I saw this little green statue of an Indian with a bow and arrow in his hands, getting ready to let fly at the sky. "What in the heck is that?" I asked a security guard.

"That's the new statue for the top of the Statehouse," he said. "We're going to reinforce the dome, make a bigger Indian—this is just a model—and put it at the very top."

"A green Indian?" I asked.

"Well, I guess it'll turn green after a while."

"Yeah," I said, "and it won't be green from envy, I know that."

You see, folks, I've seen green Indians before. When I was growing up, you could still find those old Indian-head pennies. You'd be walking along down some Kansas dirt road, and you'd see something the color of a stagnant pond. You'd dig it up, rub it off, and an Indian would appear under your thumb. Now, I suspect that's where the U.S. Government wanted the American Indian: right under its thumb. Later on, of course, there was the nickel with the Indian on one side, the buffalo on the other. "Kill one," General Phil Sheridan said, "and you kill the other." The Government wanted them both extinct at the same time, and darn near succeeded, with the help of many a private citizen, Kansans included.

Now, that's just a sad chapter in American history, from long ago. Or at least so I thought until I saw that little green statue in the Statehouse. There was that Indian, buck naked except for a breechcloth, a nose shaped like a tomahawk, like the noses of the character actors who played American Indians in the movies all through the '30s and '40s. And this Indian was standing there, shooting an arrow into the sky, like he was thinking about the Kansas motto, "To the Stars Through Difficulties." Folks, I'll give you an Indian head penny for every time an Indian thought about the Kansas State Motto. And I'll give you another for every time he shot an arrow straight up just for the hell of it. Arrows were too precious. It was white folks made up the verse I had to learn in grade school: "I shot an arrow into the air/ It fell to earth I knew not where." An Indian, you see, is too smart to lose track of an arrow.

So what's happened? Why in God's name are we putting an Indian on top of the Statehouse? And why, if we're going to do it, did we agree on a model that shows us every white man's cliche about Native Americans, from the breechcloth (which Plains Indians would have seldom worn) to the bow and arrow (you know most Indians in Kansas were also agricultural). Why did the Kansas Arts Commission agree on this design, when it has all the originality of the Indian Head Penny, or the Big Chief Tablet? And did anyone ask one of the tribes what they thought of it?

I'm old, folks, and maybe just a little cranky. But I've noticed some things in my long life, and I want you to think about this: In what state are you when they name something after you? The answer: Usually dead. In what state are you when they put your face on something? Usually dead. Or when they create a monument to you? Usually dead. Believe me, once you start getting celebrated, be careful: You're on your way out.

Think of this: Kansas has twelve counties named for Indian tribes, but Indian lands in only two counties, and none of the reservations any bigger than a legislator's brain. Indian history takes up about half a chapter of Kansas history books, lumped in with geography and flora and fauna. You could take what most Kansans know about Indians and dance it on the edge of a nickel.

And believe me, this statue won't help. Sure, it honors our past. Maybe it gives a nod to the simple fact we stole the land we live on from the Native American. Maybe it admits that Native Americans are Kansans, too. But if you think about it, you got to admit, it does those things in the worst kind of way. If I was an Indian, I'd be mad. And I wouldn't just be shooting my arrows into the air, thinking about the Kansas motto.

Here, Kansans Aren't Sure About the Humanities

We all share a need to make sense of our lives, to understand and contribute to the world around us. The humanities answer this need by offering us ways to interpret the past and imagine the future. Through history, philosophy, literature and related areas of thought, we connect our lives to the rich pattern of human experience.
—Kansas Humanities Council, Mission Statement

A wise man will not go out of his way for information.
—Henry David Thoreau

Folks, I'm always mighty glad when the legislature forks over a little funding for the Kansas Humanities Council. And what is this Kansas Humanities Council? you ask. That's what we in Here, Kansas, wanted to know one summer.

You see, I was teetering down to the Co-op when Mabel Beemer waved. "Mr. Oleander. Did you hear? The humanitarians are coming to town."

"Who the heck are they?" I asked. "Rotarians that act human?"

On the next block Elmer Peterson jumped out of the Here Drive-Thru Pharmacy and Car Wash. "Did you hear?" he asked. "Somebody from some humane society in Topeka is lecturing. They got what they call a Speaker's Bureau and they'll send somebody anywhere in the state to talk. And for nothing."

"Well," I said, "I've always heard talk was cheap."

"Especially if you're a baby chicken," Elmer said to my back.

In front of the Co-op, William "Bill of Rights" Leidecker, Here's only radical, stood arguing with

Hattie and Tommy Burns—they run the Here College of Beauty and Fiberglass Maintenance. Hattie was hot. "You're the only one in Here would invite a secular humanist to pollute our minds," she shrieked at "Bill of Rights."

"They ain't secular humanists, they're sexual humanists," Tommy interrupted. "I read that same article in the so-called Chronicle of Higher Education. They're lowering education, if you ask me."

"They ain't either one," said Bill. "It's one humanist, from the Kansas Humanities Council, and this humanist is a she."

"I don't care what you say," said Hattie. "It's a Godless atheist come to poison our minds, and the minds of our children."

"Who in Here has children?" asked Bill. "Let alone a mind to poison?"

I walked on into the Co-op. "I think we ought to boycott them right out of Here," said Claude Anderson. "Bill didn't ask me about this humanities pogrom. Do you know what a pogrom is? It's where they get rid of you if you don't agree with them. And they'll be in Here, tonight!"

Folks, Here buzzed all day. Until six o'clock, when a little foreign car cruised real slow down Kansas Street, turned around, cruised back through, turned around again, then stopped in front of the Mini-mart. A normal-looking woman, who happened to be a humanist, climbed out and asked for directions.

Half the town, about 18 folks, showed up for her lecture. We all sat and listened. That woman talked about women's history, which is what women seem best at these days, something about my grandmother being a lady but working like a dog. It didn't sound like a humane society to me. At discussion time, Hattie stood up and said we didn't need Godless humanists telling us what to believe. Claude stood up and asked when the pogrom would start. Elmer Peterson held up his poodle dog and asked what this woman thought of it. "Bill of Rights" wondered if society would ever change. And then the humanist drove home.

Next day Bill asked me for evaluations. "I can't say what she said, but that's the first time we've had so much of Here in one place, at one time, since the high school closed. I'm calling it a success," I said.

"Good," said Bill, "we'll do it again. "They've got a whole stable of humanists."

"How can they afford that?" I asked.

"Government money," said Bill.

"Then bless the Kansas Humanities Council and their programs," I said. "It's not often we get anything from the government that doesn't either make paperwork or make us spit. Why, for the next one, I might even drive to Wichita and get me a new battery for my hearing aid."

Here, Kansans Aren't Sure About Black History Month

> *For Afro-Americans, Kansas represented something that Nebraska and the Dakotas did not. Kansas was the land of John Brown, "a free state in which a colored man can enjoy his freedom." He could prosper under his own vine and fig tree and watch his children grow up free and educated. ... Kansans ... held out precisely the same welcome to Black settlers as to white.*
> *—Nell Irvin Painter, Exodusters*

Just when you think the Ku Klux Klan is dead in Kansas, you read about a Klan rally in Topeka. And it's only once a year that the newspapers decide to tell you about African-Americans in Kansas—and that's because it's Black History Month. One year, William "Bill of Rights" Liedicker, the Here, Kansan who cares most deeply about social justice, equality and human rights, decided it was time for Here to celebrate black America.

"Nicodemus Blake is the only black in Here," muttered Claude Anderson. "And he doesn't celebrate it. Why celebrate what we have so little of?"

"There's mighty little of mountains and igloos, Greek gods and whales," answered "Bill of Rights," "yet our children learn of them in the consolidated school. Sadly, they do not study black history."

"They study Kansas history," I said. I told "Bill of Rights" about the Bleeding Kansas/John Brown days, when the anti-slavery abolitionists fought the Pro-slavery Missouri Bushwhackers. We entered the Union with a free-state constitution. During the Civil War, Kansas gave as many lives to the Union per capita as any other state. After the war, thousands of black "Exodusters" migrated out of the Reconstruction South to find freedom in Kansas. I reminded him of Brown vs. the Topeka Board of Education, which led to the national desegregation of schools. "They learn all of that," I said, and rested my case.

"Sure," said "Bill of Rights." "They learn all the good little white lies of history." He told me many anti-slavery people just wanted to live where there were no blacks. That our free-state constitution gave no legal rights to free blacks. That most of the Exodusters found themselves crowded into Kansas City, Lawrence and Topeka, with few resources and less help. He wondered why we should celebrate Brown vs. Board when it proved again our segregated past, and when the Topeka folks have spent millions of dollars ever since defending their gerrymandered and still-racist school district boundaries.

"Well, I don't see it that way," I said. "I'm not cynical."

But you know, folks, by then it seemed odd to me that two old white men in an all-white town were facing off about the racial history of Kansas.

So I went home and called Nicodemus Blake. And he brought me some books to read. In Langston Hughes' novel Not Without Laughter, the young black protagonist says to his grandmother: "I guess Kansas is getting like the South . . . They don't like us here either, do they?"

Gordon Parks, in The Learning Tree, writes: "Like all other Kansas towns, Cherokee Flats wallowed in the social complexities of a borderline state. . . . The law books stood for equal rights, but the law . . . never bothered to enforce such laws in such books . . ."

Frank Marshall Davis, in his autobiography Livin' The Blues, writes about his graduation evening at Arkansas City High School: "Although I am six feet one and weigh 190 at the age of seventeen, I feel more like one foot six; for I am black, and inferiority has been hammered into me at school and in my daily life away from home."

I returned the books to Nicodemus Blake, shook his hand, and apologized for my ignorance. Then I went and found William "Bill of Rights" Liedicker in the Co-op. "Seems like most blacks would agree with you," I said. "Nicodemus gave me some reading. Seems like Kansas has a long ways to go. Maybe we do need to think about Black History Month in Here."

"Bill of Rights" smiled. "You have thought," he said. "You have sought advice from Nicodemus. You have learned. And isn't that what Black History Month is for?"

"Nope," I said. "It's for celebration. I believe we've failed again."

"Ah," said "Bill of Rights" Leidicker, "true Kansans always!"

Here, Kansans Aren't Sure About the War Against Drugs

In Here, Kansas, we're skeptical of folks trying to fix up our behavior. One time, back before World War I—it was just after Carry A. Nation reminded Kansans that we weren't exactly obeying the Prohibition laws—a hatchet-faced man visited the Here Grade School. This Temperance worker took two drinking glasses, and four worms, and put two worms in each glass. He poured water into one glass, whiskey into the other. He talked an hour while we kids fidgeted, then he had us study the drinking glasses. The worms in the water were as squirmy as we were. The ones in the whiskey were pale and limp, dead and pickled. "What do you suppose we may deduce from this demonstration?" the Temperance worker asked.

Claude Anderson, who went on to have a distinguished career as a Probate Judge in Here, raised his hand. "It shows if you drink whiskey, you won't have worms," he said.

We busted up laughing, and that thin Temperance man left the Here Grade School defeated.

I thought of that the other day when a foot soldier in the War Against Drugs showed up in Here, Kansas: my great-great-grandson, a second-grader from Topeka. He brought him a plastic Frisbee ring that glows in the dark like a halo. On it, bold, black words announce: "I am going to say NO to drugs and alcohol." Me and the boy tossed the Frisbee a few times, then went inside to rest.

I opened the icebox and pulled out a beer. "What is that, Grandpa Oleander?" the boy asked.

"Beer," I said, popping the can. "Miller High Life."

"Did you know beer is a drug?" he asked. "Did you know drugs hurt your self-esteem? Did you know drugs are dangerous? You can get hooked. You can end up without any money, or family, or friends. You end up doing anything just to get it."

"Well, Sonny," I said, "I hear that's true. But I'm over ninety years old, and I don't have to do anything to get it but open the icebox and pull out a can."

"You could just say no, like I do," he said.

"Maybe I will," I said, taking a swig of beer. "Maybe tomorrow."

"I will," Sonny said. "Tomorrow and every day. I'm living my whole life drug-free."

"Good," I said. I pulled out my chewing tobacco and gnawed off a little hunk. I settled it in my mouth where it wouldn't bother my beer.

"What's that?" asked Sonny. And I told him. "It's a drug," he concluded. "It's a drug, too."

He was right, and he was concerned.

You know, his momma had a hell of a time putting him to sleep that night on account of all his questions about my drug use: my two cans of High Life, my hour with my cud.

"I'm sorry," his mother said when she finally had him asleep.

"I don't blame the little guy for being puzzled," I said. And I didn't. You know, they brainwash these kids instead of letting them think. They tell them the easy thing, with the word JUST in there as though life was simple. Then everywhere a kid looks, the adult world is hooked: if not on drugs or alcohol or tobacco, then on television, on making money, on fast food, on credit cards, on shopping malls, on the pleasures of now instead of life lived for the future. If you don't believe me, figure the national debt on your fingers, or find the dollars lost in the savings-and-loan scandals.

The whole damn nation won't say no to drugs, or to greed, or to material accumulation, or to whatever fix makes us feel good for a moment. And we expect kids like Sonny, asleep in Here, Kansas, with his wrinkled-up face, to say no. To "JUST say no." To save themselves. Maybe even to save us.

And so he's puzzled.

I don't blame him.

Here, Kansans Aren't Sure About State Tourism

Well, my great-grandson came to Kansas for a visit. My boy and I drove all the way to Kansas City to pick him up at the International Airport. Tell me what's international about a bunch of cement where there used to be corn fields, unless the whole damn world is backed up to the ass end of a concrete truck. Sometimes I wonder. Makes me glad I've lived in rural Kansas all my life.

Anyway, we were headed back to God's country when my great- grandson asked us to pull over under a banner: "Get your free Coleman cooler," it said. He went inside a concrete hut and came out with a booklet. "Linger Longer," it said. Inside, it told us how to linger.

"I've lingered in this damn state my whole life," I told him. "Go in and get me my cooler."

"Bad news," he said. "This is for out-of-staters only. To get us to do things. Four things and I've got my cooler. Might as well. I'll be here a week." He opened his booklet. "I need one motel, hotel, or campground sticker, one attraction sticker, and two restaurant/specialty shop stickers.

This whole book's full of places to stay, things to do, neat places to eat and shop. This'll be fun."

"You're going to be in Here, Kansas," I reminded him.

He looked up Here. Nothing. He looked up Near Here. Nothing. We found one campground fifty miles from Here. "I'll go up there and fish one night," he said. He was happy as a bug looking through the booklet. Fact is, he spent so much time with the fine print he missed Eastern Kansas before he ever looked up.

"You mean we're past Topeka?" he asked. He was kinda mad the booklet was in alphabetical order. He hadn't got to the "T's" yet.

"You're going to have to look sharp," I said.

And he did. The rest of the trip home he compared where we were headed with what was in the book. We stopped at two Vista restaurants—Kansas-based fast food. I don't know where they were, some place in cement-land Kansas. Toward evening he had a powerful yearning to stay at a Holiday Inn and get his little sticker, but we were only two hours from Here, and we said no.

You know, it was hell keeping that boy in Here, Kansas. "Can we go get a sticker today?" he'd ask every day before he even said "Good morning."

Finally, we turned him loose to get his attraction sticker. He came back that night needing a tank of gas and a good night's sleep. Then a couple days later he went to a campground for the night and fished a little instead of seeing his Aunt Pearl who drove in from Wichita especially on account of him.

By the time his Kansas vacation was over, he had that Linger Longer booklet memorized. We drove him to the airport and he'd see a sign for Fort Larned, or the Cosmosphere, or the Combat Air Museum, and say, "That's in my book. I could have stopped there."

At the turnpike exit, he filled out the forms, and dropped off his page of stickers. They told him to allow four to six weeks for delivery. He was awful proud of the picture he'd seen of that plastic cooler.

Well, me and my son headed home. We would have liked to have seen more of that boy,

110

but then he was off lingering longer. You know, after two restaurants, a campground fee and fishing license, admission to his attraction, and gasoline for my car, he spent about $50 on that cooler. On our way home, me and my son bought a cooler at K-Mart for $7.95, cooled a $3.00 six-pack of beer, and cruised to Here on the back roads, letting our eyes linger on beautiful Kansas scenery the whole damn way.

Folks, you can still get a Coleman cooler in Kansas. Now, they call it "Secrets," though why you'd want to base a whole state-wide tourism program on secrets, I'll never know. Anyway, here's one secret you probably already know: Don't come to Here, Kansas, for your little stickers. We don't have a motel, a restaurant or an attraction. What do we have? Plenty of Kansas, and all of it free.

Here, Kansans Aren't Sure About "Kansas Food" Unless They Grow It Themselves

*Now potatoes they grow small in
      Kansas,*
*Potatoes they grow small in
      Kansas;*
*Potatoes they grow small, they
      dig them in the fall,*
*And eat them hide and all, in
      Kansas*
—Kansas folksong, "In Kansas"

The other day I hobbled into the Here, Kansas, Mini-Mart and young Claude Hopkins sang out, "Mr. Oleander, come check out these cantaloupe. Fresh in from down at Wichita."

I took a look. They were little things, greener than a fresh cow pie, and they didn't smell much better. I turned on my heels and walked away. "Wait," yelled Claude, "look at the box. Those are melons from the land of Kansas!"

I waved my hand in the air. I'd seen the little decal from the State Board of Agriculture: that half sunflower, half rising sun, designed to make us all patriotic eaters. I wasn't going to buy and eat a hard Wichita melon just because it was from Kansas.

My father was a farmer back in the days when 90 percent of what you put into your farm was labor. Now, you see, it's about 10 percent labor. Your other 90 percent is a banker in a pinstripe suit. Time was money to my father, even though he didn't have much of either, but I remember his acre of cantaloupe ripening through a Kansas summer. Every morning while he was milking our one cow, Eastern Capital, he'd set his little banty rooster loose in the melons. By the time milking was done, that little rooster would just be fixing to lay into a melon. That's the one my father'd pick for our breakfast. Same thing with strawberries. He'd watch the patch every day until the birds hovered like buzzards. "Okay," he'd say when one finally swooped for a strawberry, "go get them before the birds do."

Same thing with tomatoes and corn. Nowadays, even in the Land of Ah's, in the land of Kansas: Say it Above a Whisper, in the land of The Secret's Out!, in this great agricultural state, the tomatoes are gassed worse than a World War I veteran. The corn is drier than an old man's hangnail. Back when we farmed, we didn't have to call our tomatoes vine-ripened. Of course they were. Our tomatoes and corn were raccoon-ripened. My father would pull me into the garden and show me little coon tracks, show me where they'd taken a good bite out of a sweet juicy tomato, or stripped the husk off the sweetest ear of corn. "You watch how the coon picks what he wants," my father would say. "Pay attention. Remember, a coon has more time than you and me. A coon is smarter than us on this thing."

Well, it don't take a raccoon to tell me that most of the produce down at the Mini-Mart wouldn't tempt a starving man. It may be grown in Kansas soil, but I bet the seed is imported out of laboratories God knows where. The soil is fertilized with imported chemicals, protected by insecticides and fungicides and herbicides, picked by city-manufactured machines way too early, covered with paraffin so you'd think you were eating a birthday candle to get the frosting, and bruised, bruised, bruised in shipment from Wichita or Topeka or Kansas City.

I got the same beef about Kansas beef. Tell me how it's different from Argentine beef: same controlled genetics, same dinky feed lots making Kansas smell like the whole state is dying, same chemicals—from steroids to antibiotics—same cuts, same packaging. Except that little decal on the package.

That little symbol has nothing to do with

food, it has to do with money. I got nothing against the economics of buying Kansas, I just don't like it confused with quality. Because when it comes right down to it, there ain't much purely Kansas food.

Except, that is, in Here, Kansas. You come visit me, and we'll go down to No-Mile Creek and forage some sunflower seeds and bird eggs. Then we'll pull that road-kill possum out of my freezer. Trust me, I know he's a real Kansas possum, even though he didn't come with his little decal from the Kansas State Board of Agriculture.

And we've got other things in Here that don't have a decal. Especially in summer, when all of us celebrate how that season tastes in Here, Kansas. Let me explain. You see, during those weeks through the winter and early spring, when young Claude Hopkins tries to tempt us old folks with the limp, colorless, nearly-ripe produce shipped to the Here Mini-Mart—yes, through those long, cold months, we resist temptation. We could buy and eat a gassed tomato, or a head of lettuce that's travelled to us farther than a penitent on a pilgrimage; we could munch on an overgrown California carrot so woody it would break a rabbit's tooth.

But we don't. And we won't. Because we know, come spring, that the real thing—vegetables grown in the soil all around Here—will be available, and it won't taste like the inside of someone's shoe. We wait for that happy day when someone, usually Hattie Burns, shows up at the Co-op with the thin, tender leaves of Simpson lettuce—grown from plants she started in a cold frame way back on Valentine's Day.

Seems like each of us in Here has our specialty. After Hattie's lettuce, it isn't long before Claude Anderson comes in with a fistful of baby carrots; they sprout out of his hand like little fingers. They're so sweetly soft they melt in our mouths like taffy.

From there, it's Mabel Beemer's beets, each the size of a golf ball, the red-veined greens for salad, the purple ball for boiling, peeling, slicing: then the taste of the sweet earth itself.

Next, Tommy Burns is in the Co-op one morning with a sack full of new potatoes. We each grab a few for that first potent starch, for the slightly-sour taste of the thin skin as it peels back during steaming, for the rich buttery flavor of potato meat like you can't buy at the Mini-Mart.

Of course tomatoes are everyone's pleasure, and the difference between home-grown and store-bought is the difference between lightning and the lightning bug (as Mark Twain used to say about choosing the right word). But words can't describe the acidic sweetness, the tender flesh, the bursting ooze of juice in a home-grown tomato. Words don't have to, because it's enough for the tongue simply to have the taste lingering there. And I hate to brag, but I have brought in the first taste of tomatoes for the past two years, right around July 4th, and I've had the earliest taste in my own back yard.

Of course sweet corn comes next. That's Elmer Peterson's specialty. But he won't let you taste it unless you follow his ritual. He comes to the Co-op of a morning, beaming. "It's time," he says. That evening, we show up at his house around six, just as we're ready to make a vegetable the last of our suppers. We wait next to his garden. Suddenly Elmer sprints out of his kitchen with a big pot of boiling water, yelling "Let's go." Each of us grabs an ear he's X-ed with a magic marker. We quickly shuck it, we drop it in the pot, and in less than five minutes we're all of us standing in Elmer's garden eating the sweetest, most tender, most glorious corn we've ever tasted.

Folks, it's worth the wait. There's something about a garden. And in Here, Kansas, we're like Adam and Eve: if we're going to be tempted, it'll be in a garden, and not in some hellish Mini-Mart.

Here, Kansans Share Their Secrets For a Long Life—Just Call

> *He reads the papers on the porch,*
> *concentrates on the obits.*
> *There're people dying now*
> *that ain't never died before,*
> *he says, and looks at me*
> *like I'm some hope,*
> *or could raise the dead.*
> — *David Ewick,*
> *"Grandfather on the Porch"*

The Wichita paper heard that all these little Kansas towns are full of old folks. They found them a cub reporter, and put him on assignment: Go get their secrets.

So last week this kid drives into Here, Kansas, in a little Honda, cruising Kansas Street looking for canes, crutches, and walkers, for worn overalls, bald heads and blue hair. Course it was hot, and all of us were in the Co-op playing checkers and remembering how to spit: "It's what you used to do before you started drooling," Claude Anderson teased me.

"It's drool with a little force," said Tommy Burns.

And then that young reporter walked in. He was already pudgy in the middle from too much beer. He wore cowboy boots. He whipped out pencil and notebook, explained his mission, and hurried us with questions.

Wilbur Schlingensiepen gave me a wink. "Son," he said, "never be in a hurry. Look how you walked in here and hustled out your notebook. Old folks learn to deal with time. The faster you go, the shorter your life." The young man wrote that down fast as he could. "You see, son," Wilbur went on, "life is a journey. You want the journey to last, you go slow. You want the journey over, you go fast. No different from driving to California. You got that?"

"I got it," the boy gulped.

"And never wear cowboy boots," I said. "The boots ruin your feet, give you the arthritis, you end up sitting too much, then you get a stomach on you and die young. Me, I wear wide shoes and walk after every meal."

"Never drive a foreign car," said Claude Anderson. "Ever notice how they always smell new? Well, they put something in so the air is bad. It's deteriorating the health of Americans something awful. You ever find an old Chevy that smells new?"

Well, folks, after we teased him with everything we could see about him, we started in on ourselves. There's no secret to old age, but you ask an old person and he'll tell you his habits, or she'll tell you what to avoid. Why, Mabel Beemer, in the Co-op for glue, said, "You must keep a garden. It's some growing thing that needs you every livelong day."

"No," said William "Bill of Rights" Leidecker, "fighting the world keeps you young. This country has kept me alive. I fought the old law against German in schools, and alcohol prohibitions, and income taxes. I've burned the flag to show my fight."

"One drink every day," I said. "Red, not white, wine."

"Drinking," said Claude Anderson, "will pickle your liver."

"Never travel," said Tommy Burns. "You pick up germs."

"Travel," said Nicodemus Blake. "It keeps you young, broadens your mind. But don't drink unfiltered water."

"And one dose of blackstrap molasses every livelong day," said Mabel Beemer. "And no tight-fitting jeans."

"No clothes that don't breathe," said Claude Anderson. "Your whole body needs to breathe. Going naked at home is best."

Maybe it was the prospect of Claude

Anderson, nude, but by that time we were talking to our ancient selves. That young reporter had hopped into his foreign car and sped away, in a hurry to get to Wichita and write up all our good advice.

But folks, these days you don't have to actually drive to Here to get some advice, to talk with someone old enough to be your grandma's grandpa. That's because, some time ago, Economic Development hit Here, Kansas. Let me explain:

I was in the Co-op, drinking coffee with Elmer Peterson, of the Drive-Thru Pharmacy and Car Wash, and Barney Barnhill, of Here's Demolition Derby Museum. Mabel Beemer was shopping for an air freshener, which Claude Anderson didn't have. She huffed out, saying, "Your pharmacy didn't have my brand either, Elmer. But that's all right, my son's driving me to Wichita next Sunday."

An angry Claude Anderson swept from behind the counter and slammed the door after Mabel. Then he turned on us. "Get out!" he yelled. "You come in and buy your nickel cup of coffee, and use up the air-conditioning I have to pay for. I'm going bankrupt."

When he calmed down, we talked small-town economics. Elmer admitted that only Medicaid was keeping him open. Barney Barnhill can't even make beer money displaying Demolition Derby cars. We thanked God for Social Security. "Social Security might keep us alive," said Claude, "but it won't keep our businesses open."

That's when Tommy Burns came in. "We need a consultant," he said. Now, beware: Anyone who recommends a consultant is usually related to one. And, sure enough, Tommie went on, "My nephew's a whiz on economic development. Part of this Kansas Main Street Program. Success everywhere he goes."

So Bobby Burns came to town. He asked for a tour. We gave him one.

Two minutes later he was drinking coffee in the Co-op and thinking. "This kind of your hangout?" he asked.

Most days, we told him.

"And you have a phone line in here?"

Claude said yes.

"You think you could stay open into the evenings? Even into the night a ways?" he asked.

"Can't sell gas then, said Claude. "Nobody in Here drives after dark."

"I'm not talking gas," said Bobby Burns. And then he outlined his vision for Eco Devo in Here. "All across America," he said, "people are awake at night, and they've had hard days, and their kids are wringing them out, and they know they're watching too much television, and they don't have church anymore, and they don't have family close by. They need Here, Kansas. They need an older voice. They need Dial-A-Geezer."

Folks, I don't want to turn this into a commercial, but when you finish reading this, go to your telephone and dial 1-900- GRANDPA. Someone will answer—maybe me, or Claude, or Elmer, or Tommy, or Barney. Whoever's on shift.

Or if you want to talk to Mabel Beemer, or Hattie Burns, or Minnie Small, dial 1-900- GRANDMA. That's 1-900-472-6362 or 1-900-472-6372.

Yes, for only $1.99 a minute, a nice, grandmotherly voice will say, "Honey, your grandfather used to be the same way." Or, "They say patience is a virtue, but it's not my virtue." Or, "I have a mind to bake you a big batch of cookies, right now."

Or you might want something grandfatherly: "Better to fix the fence than kill the pig that got loose." Or, "If you're gonna chew, you gotta spit." Yes, we promise to soothe your woes and griefs with "Uhmm-hummm," and "Sure, sure," and "That's right, that's right." You'll feel better in minutes. We will, too, because ever since Dial-A-Geezer, folks in Here are down at the Co-op, all hours, fighting over the phone. And not one of us cares whether Claude Anderson does or does not stock Mabel Beemer's air freshener.

Here, Kansans and Their Courtship Rituals

—adapted from Paul I. Wellman, Bowl of Brass

*So come all you girls and listen
to my noise,
Don't you never marry no
Kansas boys,
If you do your fortune it will be:
Hoe-cakes, hominy, sassafras tea
—"Kansas Boys,"
Kansas folksong*

When I was a boy in Here, a fellow named Jake walked the streets looking just like he'd climbed off a horse in Dodge City: his legs were bowed and he shuffled like it was a misery to be on foot instead of horseback. He always wore gloves; a kerchief at his neck was his only concession to color. Jake was a quiet man. His only greeting was a shy nod of the head, his most effusive gesture an awkward handshake, his momentary smile the only way you'd know he'd gotten your joke. He looked like a lot of old Kansas ranch bachelors, men more comfortable with horses and cows than women.

But Jake was no bachelor. He was married to the effusive musical director of the Here First Methodist Church, a woman whose refinement, musical taste, easy manners, and conversational skills made every woman in Here either jealous or a copycat. Rose had been raised in the East, attended finishing school, and she represented all of Here's aspirations. We young folks wondered how the two of them had ever found each other, and the courtship story of refined Rose and cowboy Jake is Here legend.

Seems that Rose came from Boston to visit relatives in Here one summer. She impressed everyone in town, singing at the church, hosting teas with her Aunt Maudie, playing piano and talking suffrage. On her last day with her aunt and uncle, they overslept. Half dishevelled, and panting, they ran the several blocks to the train station. They missed the train. Rose began to cry as though it were the last train that would ever run from Kansas.

"Nope," said the station master, "just catch the eastbound from Lindsborg. That's about four hours from Here in a wagon. Train don't leave there for another six hours. Plenty of time." Herman shook his head, wondering where he was going to find the buggy, and a good horse. That's when he saw Jake.

Aunt Maudie and Uncle Herman knew all about Jake, a boy who'd lost his parents and been raised by cowboys out on a ranch. Back then Jake was a tall, gangly boy who'd never been around women, and he stammered and shook and found new shades of red-in- the-face to turn even when in the presence of the coarse waitresses down at the Eat and Leave Cafe. Seems Jake was at the depot signing papers at the Santa Fe office when Maudie and Herman and Rose ran up to ask him the favor: Would he take the young woman to Lindsborg?

Jake was so shocked he couldn't say no, so flustered he could hardly look at Rose, so embarrassed he could only trace a wide circle with the toe of his boot on the depot floor. He was recruited.

"Let's all go home for a nice breakfast, since we missed it in our rush," said Maudie.

That's when Jake made his second mistake. Maudie served some eggs, and fried up some leftover potatoes, and since Jake didn't want to talk, he ate instead. Rose did, too, maybe nervous herself about her unsure travel plans.

After breakfast, Jake brought around his horse and buckboard, and they loaded all of Rose's hat boxes, valises and trunks. "Why, she even had a 'portmanteau,'" Jake confessed years later to the pool hall in a rare moment of loquaciousness. Anyway, off they went.

Now, you need to know two things: First,

the countryside between Here and Lindsborg is what we Kansans courteously call "level." Second, when you fry up sour potatoes in plenty of bacon grease and salt and pepper, you can get them down, but they don't do a thing for your bowels.

Just imagine, if you will, Jake and Rose in a buckboard, Jake just as quiet as an underground stream, Rose in silent prayer that she'd make the train east, the landscape as green and level as a billiard table. And then imagine the gut-grabbing fist of sour potatoes cramping Jake's innards. Imagine Jake's terror: He knew he'd have to relieve his bowels, and soon, too, and yet that country was so level and open not even a jackrabbit could find a tumbleweed to hide behind.

Jake was brave. He put up with several waves of cramping. His eyes watered. Then another fit made Jake sweat; he darn near doubled over. That's when he had his brilliant idea. He said his first words of the trip: "Excuse me, Miss Rose, but there's a bolt loose under this here wagon, and I'd best tend to it."

Jake jumped off the buckboard, climbed underneath, and, quiet as he could, answered nature's call. He hurried back up to his seat, and giddapped his horse away from that spot. He was so relieved, so to speak, and pleased with himself, he began to talk. He told Rose about his life, about how much he loved the ranch, the land around Here, all of God's simple, but wonderful, gifts. He shouldn't have been so happy. In another half-hour he was struck from within again, and, for all his clenched teeth, he couldn't shake his urgent need. Finally, he stopped to see to the bolt under the wagon.

Relieved again, he became downright talkative, in spite of the fact Rose hadn't said a word for an hour. In fact, he gabbed away right up to when he was struck a third time by cramps so awful he could barely breathe. He stopped the wagon once more. "The bolt," he began, but he couldn't help looking at Rose's pale face, beads of perspiration rolling down her forehead, at her clenched fists, at the way she held herself stiffly in the seat.

Finally, she spoke. "Now, you listen here, Jake," she said through gritted teeth, "don't think you're the only one with a bolt loose. I'll check it this time." And she did. And when she mounted the wagon, she, too, was relieved and talkative.

Well, they travelled that way the four hours to Lindsborg, checking bolts under the wagon, telling each other about their lives, their hopes and dreams. By the time Jake put Rose on that train, they knew each other about as well as two young people can. Jake made her promise to come back, and she did. And a year later, they married.

Jake explained it down at the pool hall. "You see," he said, "when I realized that no matter how refined she was she had the same sour potatoes in her gut, and the same need to answer the call, and yet she held out for an hour longer than I could, why, how can you not admire that kind of toughness?"

Rose said the opposite: "He was just a tough young cowboy, but then he spoke so eloquently of his simple life, of the western land, of God's gifts. He was so spiritually refined, I had to admire him and his way of seeing things."

So, you see, Here has the marriage of the raw and refined, all brought together by a case of running bowels.

And the young people of Here still believe in travel during courtship. I remember a while back when Claude Anderson's young great-grandson came to him saying, "This is it. I think I'm in love."

"Think?" snorted Claude. "Don't you know?"

"How can you know?" the boy asked. "I mean, really know."

"Easy," said Claude, and he told that boy the story of Jake and Rose. "Two young folks, all alone, out in the middle of Kansas. No radio. No tapes. Running bowels," he pointed out, "are optional."

You see, folks, courtship by backroads is a double challenge. You take your average young person, raised up somewhere far away from Here, Kansas. You start from Kansas City, or Lawrence, or Manhattan, wherever the youngster might be familiar with, comfortable with. You tell your would-be partner that you're going to Here, and you're going the "scenic" route. That means it'll take six or seven hours to travel what you might do in four if you stayed on the straight and level scar that is I-70 or I-35 through Kansas. You'll cross every little creek on narrow bridges. You'll slow to 20 mph through every little two-block town. You'll play tag with trains at railroad crossing after railroad crossing. You'll slow down for unbanked curves, stall behind cattle trucks, bang your palm on the steering wheel in frustration when you're stuck behind old men like me who remember when a pickup truck couldn't do much more than 45, and don't want to test the limit beyond that.

At first, it'll seem fun. Quaint. Like having tea with your grandma and listening to her talk about her clubs. You'll show each other the fine points of scenery: a bent tree here or a hawk riding the wind there; a whole field of broom corn being swept by the wind; a stripped black feed lot dotted by white cattle. After a while, quiet sets in. If you're a true Kansan, you'll be enjoying that quiet. You'll like how the landscape grows quieter, too, as you move west.

Then you'll start watching your partner. Is she squirming? Sighing? Looking at her watch?

Rifling the glove compartment for a map? Asking you how much further it is to Here?

That's the first challenge: testing the potential partner for "Kansas tolerance." Some folks in Here say a marriage will last in direct proportion to how many miles two young people can travel the back roads to Here before they cut over to four-lane. Your lifelong partner will look up at you when you drive into Here and say, "We can't be here already!"

But there's a second challenge, too, and I'm beginning to think it's the more important one, these days: testing your own reaction to your partner's "Kansas intolerance." How do her sighing fits affect you? How long can you keep up your own spirits when hers become as gloomy as the gray sky or the wet leaves in the roadside ditches? For how long can you explain your home state, making it interesting, vital, alive—to her, and, more important, to yourself?

When Claude Anderson recommended the backroads courtship to his great-grandson, the boy said, "Why, she'd think I was crazy. I don't know, Grandpa Claude."

"Why, before I married your great-grandmother," said Claude, "I once spent fourteen hours with her in a Model A, two flat tires to repair. Twice we had to get a farmer to pull us out of the mud. We made it to Salina too late to find any of the fancy stores open. I bought her a little Christmas tree ornament at the five and dime and we came home."

"Sounds like true love, Grandpa Claude," said the boy.

"Hell, no," said Claude, "she didn't speak to me again for a year."

"Then how come you married her?"

"Because when she did speak, right before the next Christmas, she said, 'Claude, I believe you owe me a shopping trip.' You see, boy, she was willing to travel with me again, and that made all the difference."

"Seems kind of risky," said Claude's great-grandson. "I don't want to risk my relationship all in one trip."

Claude just hooted. "Nothing," he said, "is riskier than love."

Turned out both Claude and the boy were right. Claude's great-grandson tried the trip and dropped the girl. Took him three young women and three trips before he found a partner he'd marry. They live in New York City now, but the stresses and strains of that bustling place don't bother them a bit: They've been tempered by the quiet of Kansas; they know they can survive anything, and survive it together, with or without running bowels.

Here, Kansans Are Never Too Old For Love and Independence

I was out in my yard raking leaves on a sixty-degree day one February not so long ago. Just below the crust of leaves, I uncovered the pale green, tender, upthrust shoots of daffodil, iris, jonquil and crocus. All around Here, Kansas, the smallest shreds of grass were greening, the lilac buds were swelling, sap was rising. I love Kansas, because often, in February, you see that little bit of spring in the middle of what ought to be a frigid winter.

It doesn't seem natural, but I never complain. Nope, on those nice days I go outside. On those nice nights, I put on an old, thin sweater and head over to the Near Here VFW with Elmer Peterson to play a little bingo.

Well, this particular February (it will forever be etched in my memory), I bought four cards, and sat down to win something. After five rounds of near bingos, I gave my cards one last chance on a blackout. The round began, and the tension built like it does in blackout, so you know someone has to win with every new call: I-20, or B-9. I lacked all but two O's when a woman in the palest green dress I'd ever seen suddenly stood up.

"Bingo," she called out in a strong voice. She carried her card, not so much walking as floating, to the front.

"Who's that?" I whispered to Elmer. She was a young woman, not more than 80, her white hair in a loose bun, her eyes brighter than you could polish a Roosevelt dime. Like her voice, the rest of her was all tender strength. She was spring in a winter of old people and regulars at the VFW. And my sap rose.

"Winner of blackout," the caller announced, "is Miss Iola Humboldt."

Miss Humboldt whispered to the caller, and he said: "Iola has just moved to Near Here from southeast Kansas to be near her niece, . . ." And I missed her niece's name.

I poked Elmer. "What was her niece's name?"

"William," he said, "you'll find out all about her in good time."

"At my age, time ain't that good," I said.

I picked up my cards and headed to where I'd seen her stand up. She was heading back, too, and we met in front of two empty folding chairs. Her smell came to me, like a faint reminder of lilac. Her face was soft, wrinkled, and worn—but gently, like a map you've used over and over to get where you want to go. My face flushed pink as a crabapple blossom, and I went where I wanted to go. "May I join you?" I asked. "These cards need some extra luck."

She smiled, and sat. Her hand reached for mine. "Please join me," she said with no hesitation. "But at our age," she said, "we don't want to count on luck."

Folks, I don't need to tell you how bingo didn't matter anymore that evening: Those little plastic flaps covered the beautiful numbers like winter leaves cover what wants to grow, and I kept thinking B-9, B-9, Be-mine. I don't need to tell you how Iola Humboldt turned to me at the end of bingo and asked: "Do you believe in like at first sight?" I don't need to tell you how she invited me to supper on Valentine's Day, to get better acquainted.

I went home that night, and walked right up

to my favorite picture of my late wife, now dead these ten years. She smiled, and I smiled, too. Late in her life, she had said, "William, I no longer believe in happiness. Instead, I believe that what happens is good. I believe in happen-ness."

As my heart swelled with remembered love, and my sap rose with the thought of Iola Humboldt's hand, I knew that what was happening was good: We all deserve a little spring in winter.

But, folks, I think we also deserve some heat in summer, and after courting Iola Humboldt from Valentine's Day into June, I decided that they call July 4th Independence Day for a reason.

Now, I don't like fireworks shows: I've seen the red glare of too many rockets. I don't like firecrackers: I've seen too many kids with their fingers blown off, and an eye behind a patch. I don't much like parades: I'm happier when people march their own pace, in their own direction. But I do like independence. And I'm glad when all the old folks in Here, Kansas, celebrate the 4th in the shade of the Co-op grain elevator. We swat flies, and share the kind of potluck we're used to: old recipes for soft foods.

I invited Iola Humboldt to the Here July 4th picnic. She fried a chicken, turned over a Jell-O mold, and I picked her up at noon. We ate, and I visited with old friends while she made new ones. We sang, and we watched the few young folks throw Frisbees and sweat. We talked wheat harvest (not very good), livestock prices (not very good), and weather (not very good). We let the sun set.

When the whole night sky was shot through with stars, I put my arm around Iola Humboldt's shoulder. I caressed the little knob her shoulder blade made.

"Iola," I said, "look at those stars. They're the only thing in Here, Kansas, much older than I am. But I'm still young enough to feel impetuous. Iola," I whispered, "I want you to come live with me. In my house. Will you?"

She took a deep breath. She let it out so slow my heart stopped. "William," she said, "whatever makes you think a couple of old birds like us will get along cooped up in the same little house?"

"Who said anything about getting along?" I asked. "I asked you to come live with me. I want to sit on the porch at night and not have to worry about driving you home. I want to see you first thing in the morning, when my back's so stiff I can't think of a single good reason to get out of bed. I want to feel your knobby old shoulders when we watch TV on the couch. And maybe we'll like bickering and disagreeing with each other as much as we like getting along. Will you do it? Will you talk with your daughter about it?"

"I will not," she said.

Folks, my heart bounced in my chest then.

Until Iola continued. "I don't need to," she said. "It's Independence Day, and I'm an independent woman. Pick me up first thing in the morning. I'll have my things packed." And she kissed my cheek.

July 5th, I was up before dawn, pacing. I couldn't eat breakfast. Finally, when the stars quieted down with the promise of sunrise, I started the drive between Here and Near Here. Halfway there, I stopped the car, suddenly unsure of what I was doing. The sun, that big star, lifted off the eastern horizon. And, between it and me, was an abandoned building, somebody's first homestead house, I can't remember whose. With the sun behind it, every crack glowed, every shattered window sparkled. The whole thing was shot through with so much light it looked like it might explode. It was beautiful, more beautiful than a snug bungalow or a patched outbuilding or a painted barn. It was old, and decrepit, and useless. But it was awful good for holding sunlight, for glowing in the morning, for radiating light.

And you know what? Iola Humboldt was ready and waiting when I pulled into her drive.

Here, Kansans Know How to Celebrate Thanksgiving Day

How did you spend your Thanksgiving, the ladies of our Church gave a thanksgiving dinner at one of the halls and festival in the evening. ... There was a young fell [sic] called in a Splendid two horse Barouche, to take our things to the church so I got a splendid chance to ride to the hall. As we were ready to walk home Jen and I ... borrowed another Barouche from one of the ladies of our church, and invited a young Dr. to drive us home. Now ... please don't consider me fast, or what is usually termed crazy after the fells, for I am neithur [sic], I see it does not do for school girls to let their minds run thus at too great an extent, but it is thanksgiving time now ...
—Ovella Dunn,
letter to friend, 1870

Just like most Americans, Iola Humboldt and I visited family over Thanksgiving. We stopped first at Wichita's Hilltop Countryside Manor Retirement Home.

"There goes my appetite," I told Iola. At my age, when a smell hits me, you know it's pretty strong. An exasperated woman at the front desk nodded toward the dining room when we asked after my cousin Robert. We'd already decided not to share dinner with Robert: Who wants Thanksgiving food prepared by people who don't care about you? But Robert wasn't in the dining room. He sat in front of a big-screen TV, staring blankly at a football game.

Now, Robert had a very successful Allis-Chalmers dealership up in There, Kansas, for years. He retired after a heart attack and bypass surgery, then got colon cancer and a colostomy. He had his stroke last year. Here's a man who once sold tractors to the stingiest farmers, who loved to travel and talk. But he's reduced to rheumy eyes, patchy shaves, and single syllables.

Still, he knew who we were. He grinned at

the television as though to apologize. With his right hand he patted my knee. With his left, he held Iola's hand. Then he took us to his room. He can't write, but he'd saved greeting cards for us. We hugged him and left. "Well, the hard visit's done," I told Iola.

My Wichita grandson hosted the Oleander gathering. Even on the porch, a Thanksgiving smell hit us—turkey in the oven, pumpkin pies cooling on the sideboard. "I'm hungry again," I told Iola, and knocked on the door.

My grandson's wife looked exasperated, as though she'd already had it for the day. Children screamed through the house; the TV blared football; in the kitchen, folks shouted over each other, asking the locations of dishes, children or husbands. My grandson's wife shook her head as though to apologize, and pointed to the living room. Most of the family sat there, staring blankly at the TV. They made room on the couch.

"It's close," said a cousin.

"Great game," said another, and downed his beer.

"We visited Robert, over at the Manor," I said to nobody. I waited until a commercial. "I don't believe you've all met Iola," I said.

My great-grandson was channel-grazing with the remote, and he brought everyone the highlights of another game. I see why they call it a "remote."

We went to the kitchen. "I should have brought something," Iola said to my grandson's wife.

"It'd just go to waste," she said. "I hate Thanksgiving. Nothing but too much food and too much noise."

"That's what family's all about," I said. But she had the wrong kind of noise, and the wrong idea of food: The only noise came from TV, the only food from a kitchen where nobody cared.

Folks, I wondered why people all over America live like you *have* to live in a nursing home.

That night, Iola and I drove back to Here. We set our TV out by the curb. We fixed ourselves a little snack, not turkey, but fall vegetables from Iola's garden. We promised each other that next year, if people want to see us, they'll come to Here for loving food and no television. And then we gave thanks that we still have our brains, our appetites, our tongues, our hearts, and, better yet, the desire to use them on each other. The thanks, you see, is in the giving.

Here, Kansans Prefer Yards to Lawn, But Prefer Love Over Anything Else

What is there in a name? Mown weeds, by any other name, would smell as sweet.
—Shakesp-Here

Folks, when Iola Humboldt first moved in with me, she made changes inside the house. That was fine with me. Curtains on the windows suddenly seemed like a good idea, if you know what I mean. A new bedspread replaced the faded chintz. The old linoleum went, too. After all, it was nothing but big black stains in front of the stove, sink and refrigerator. I didn't even object when she went to Wichita and bought a soft fabric toilet seat cover with matching rug that nestles up to the stool bottom. "Easier to wash a throw rug than the floor," she said.

I hadn't noticed the dirty floor, but I held my tongue, because I know that standards for cleanliness can be different between two people. And I don't mean to paint Iola and me as some kind of "odd couple," some "Dagwood and Blondie." We've agreed to get along, to give each other room.

Then one spring I was gone to Wichita for a day and when I got home you should have seen the list of chores. And they weren't just things Iola was going to do inside the house.

The first thing on the list was, "Buy grass seed." Simple enough, I thought, until Iola said, "William, it's time we had a lawn."

"Lawn?" I asked. "What's that?" In all of my 90-plus years, I've never had a lawn. "City folks have lawns," I reminded Iola. "I've always had a yard."

"I don't care what you call it," she said. "I'm talking about a small plot of ground with more grass than weeds. That seems like a small enough request." She led me to the window and pointed to the yard. Some beautiful yellow dandelions were in flower. Crabgrass was doing its wonderful crawl out from one soggy corner. Lamb's quarter had pushed itself toward sunlight along the worn spots where my old dog, Here, used to run. Honeybees buzzed the clover blooms under the clothesline. "What do you call that?" Iola asked.

"A yard," I said. "A fine Kansas yard."

"Where's the grass?" she asked.

I shouldn't have, but I pointed vaguely out the window. "There's two blades," I said, "right next to the dwarf cherry. You see them? Or do you want the binoculars?"

"William," Iola fumed. "In southeast Kansas I had a lawn. I had one place where fescue grew a uniform green, to a uniform height. Freshly mown it was like a beautiful carpet."

"I prefer the beauty of biodiversity," I said.

"You prefer laziness to work," said Iola. "And your little jokes to helping me. Won't you do this little thing?"

"I don't know," I said. "Next you'll want to trade our screened porch for a veranda. Our patio for a deck. Our clothesline for a clothes dryer. Our compost heap for a garbage disposal. Our dishpan hands for a dishwasher. Our ... "

I shut up when Iola put her finger to my lips. "You're not planning to run for office, are you? I don't need a speech. I need a lawn."

And folks, since democracy doesn't always work in a relationship, I went out and bought some fescue. Besides, there's nothing wrong with a little bit of lawn, for Iola's sake, even if it does ruin the look of a good Kansas yard. And it never hurts to be reminded: Love, like grass, takes constant attention and care.

Here, Kansans Like Their Annual Spring Garage Sale

*People who have few possessions
cling tightly to those they have.
That is one of the facts that
make life so discouraging.
—Sherwood Anderson, "The Egg"*

Spring is the time for love and for garage sales, and I must admit I recently found the best of both at the Here, Kansas, Annual Spring Garage Sale.

Usually, our garage sales aren't much. We set out the same stuff we've been selling for the past ten years, we overprice what we secretly want to keep, we hide our change in cigar boxes underneath double-wide neckties, and we take turns going from one dark garage to another, thanking the Lord we don't own the kind of junk our neighbors do.

Of course in Here, Kansas, it's hard to be self-righteous; as soon as I get really smug pawing over Claude Anderson's display of what should be trash, I recognize it as my own, things I sold last year, or the year before that.

Fact is, in Here, Kansas, we have a small pool of folks, and the Annual Garage Sale is more like an exchange. I figure every five years I end up with the same things I sold five years before, and I'm happier for it. Let's face it, when you take a break from that claw-foot lamp, from that book of church recipes your grand-niece sent you, from that shoehorn you accidentally packed into your suitcase in 1949 at the Jayhawk Hotel in Topeka, why, all of a sudden, in somebody else's garage, in the near dark, those things look better than they have in years. And what's more, they're cheap, because Elmer Peterson is now as tired of them as you were five years ago.

But this year's Annual Spring Garage Sale was just a little different. Pierre Small, president of the Here, Kansas, DENSA Society, that support group for the dull-witted, the dizzy and the dense, helped organize our efforts. Someone suggested a bake sale to fill the DENSA treasury, and he got the whole community together for what he called the DENSA Half-Baked Sale.

People brought failed cookies—doughy and burned; cakes— fallen, crumpled, and only partially iced; brownies—like hardtack; crumbly fudge; breads that refused to rise. The food was terrible, but you have to admit that DENSA is a wonderful cause. And Pierre spent the rest of the year figuring out what to do with the few dollars we raised.

But besides the DENSA Half-Baked Sale, my garage was the hit of Here. That's because of Iola Humboldt, my newfound love. You see, people flocked to see the first influx of garage sale goods into Here, Kansas, in decades. She had crafts made at the senior center in Chanute, her former home. She had jelly jars nobody around Here has seen the likes of since the '40s. She had picture frames, flapper dresses, a clarinet, and a Ouija board. In short, she had what everybody wanted.

You know, in the rush of business I worried I wouldn't get to go out and buy all my old stuff back. Iola was tired of being cooped up, too, and I suggested she walk around Here, maybe buy a few things to revive her.

And you know what happened? While I stayed home, making change in my garage, that woman shopped and came home with everything I'd sold for the past five years. Folks, turns out Iola's taste in junk matches mine, exactly. And in Here, Kansas, at the Annual Spring Garage Sale, if that's not true love, then what the heck is?

WILLIAM JENNINGS BRYAN OLEANDER is a lifelong resident of Here, Kansas, a little town close to Near Here in There County.

Mr. Oleander spent his life as a farmer before retiring to live on Social Security and become the Honorary Mayor of Here. He has children, grandchildren, and great-grandchildren all over the state of Kansas and from the West to the East Coast. He will be 100 years old "sooner than you can count backwards to 90." He lives in a white house in Here, with his sweetheart, Iola Humboldt.

His radio commentaries about Kansas are heard twice a month on KANU, Public Radio from the University of Kansas, 91.5 FM, Lawrence, Kansas, and are published twice-monthly in the *Topeka Metro News*.

THOMAS FOX AVERILL is writer-in-residence and professor of English at Washburn University of Topeka, where he teaches courses in Creative Writing and in Kansas Literature, Folklore and Film. His books are *Passes at the Moon* (short stories), Woodley Press, 1985; *Seeing Mona Naked* (short stories), Watermark Press, 1989; *What Kansas Means to Me: Twentieth Century Writers on the Sunflower State* (essays), University Press of Kansas, 1990. In 1993, he produced a tape, Oleander's Kansas. He lives in Topeka, Kansas, with his wife, Jeffrey Ann Goudie, and his daughter, Eleanor Goudie-Averill.

PATRICK MARRIN is associate professor and chair of the Journalism Department at Benedictine College in Atchison, Kansas. He is a former editorial cartoonist for the *Topeka Capital-Journal*, the *Topeka Metro News*, and his illustration and cartoon work has appeared in newspapers and magazines both nationally and throughout Kansas. He lives in Atchison with his wife, Diane, and son, John.